Math Bugs

1st grade

Written by:

Carla Dawn Fisher & Julia Ann Hobbs

Project Directors:

Michele D. Van Leeuwen
Scott G. Van Leeuwen

Creative & Marketing Director:

George Starks

Design & Technical Project Director:

Dante J. Orazzi

TABLE OF CONTENTS

INTRODUCTION

The Math Bridge series is designed to help students improve their mathematical skills in all areas. This book has been developed to provide first grade students with skill-based exercises in the following areas: number writing, quantity, counting, estimation, comparison, place value, addition, subtraction, numerical problem solving, word problem solving, graphs, time, money, and computation. The purpose of this book, therefore, is to strengthen students' mathematical concepts, thus helping them to become better mathematicians and improve achievement test scores.

Math Bridge includes many extras to help your students in their study of mathematics. For instance,

✔ An Incentive Contract begins the book to motivate students to complete their work.

✔ A Diagnostic Test has been included to help assess your students' mathematical knowledge.

✔ Exercises become progressively more challenging as students work through the book.

✔ Tips are included throughout the book as reminders to help students successfully complete their work.

✔ Thought-provoking exercises (Brainworks) are periodically placed throughout the book to emphasize critical thinking skills.

✔ Additional exercises are included to help students in practicing with estimation.

✔ The exercises prepare students for standardized achievement tests.

✔ Each section includes problem-solving exercises written with the purpose of reinforcing the skills taught in that section.

Mathematics is all around us and is an essential part of life. It is the authors' intention that through the completion of this book, students will come away with a stronger knowledge of mathematics to assist them both inside and outside the classroom.

Incentive Contract

In • cen'tive, *n.* **1.** Something that urges a person on. **2.** Enticing. **3.** Encouraging.
4. That which excites to action or moves the mind.

LIST YOUR AGREED-UPON INCENTIVE FOR EACH SECTION BELOW
Place a ✔ after each activity upon completion

Student Signature _____

Teacher or Parent Signature _____

PG	Activity Title	✔
10	Number Writing Practice	
11	Quantity: Multiple Choice Practice	
12	Quantity: Writing Numerals	
13	Counting	
14	Comparison: Greater vs. Fewer	

MY INCENTIVE IS ✖

15	Writing from 1 to 100	
16	Before, After, Between	
17	Number Words	
18	Number Word Search	
19	Number Word Application	

MY INCENTIVE IS ✖

20	Addition Problem Solving	
21	Addition Problem Solving	
22	Mixed Equation Practice	
23	Word Problem Solving	

MY INCENTIVE IS ✖

24	Word Problem Solving	
25	Writing Equations	
26	Mixed Equation Practice	
27	Subtraction Tables	
28	Word Problem Solving	

MY INCENTIVE IS ✖

29	Mixed Application Add or Subtract	
30	Addition and Subtraction Trails	
31	Number Families	
32	Number Words	
33	Number Words: Mixed Practice	
34	Bar Graph	

MY INCENTIVE IS ✖

35	Problem Solving	
36	Matching Equations and Answers	
37	Word Problem Solving	
38	Intensive Practice	
39	Write the Sums	

MY INCENTIVE IS ✖

40	Problem Solving	
41	Matching Equations and Answers	
42	Multiple Choice Problem Solving	
43	Comparison	
44	Word Problem Solving	
45	Intensive Practice	

MY INCENTIVE IS ✖

46	Tens and Ones	
47	Tens and Ones	
48	Tens and Ones	
49	Tens and Ones	
50	Tens and Ones	

MY INCENTIVE IS ✖

51	Writing Time	
52	Drawing Clock Hands	
53	Half Hour	
54	Drawing Clock Hands	
55	Matching	
56	Writing Time	

MY INCENTIVE IS ✖

57	Counting by 2 and 5	
58	Counting Circles	
59	Counting Pennies	
60	Counting Nickels	
61	Counting Dimes	
62	Writing Numerals	

MY INCENTIVE IS ✖

63	Problem Solving	
64	Graphical Problem Solving	
65	Number Match	
66	More Problem Solving	
67	Word Problem Solving	

MY INCENTIVE IS ✖

68	Problem Solving	
69	Comparison	
70	Problem Solving	
71	Subtraction Picture	
72	Word Problem Solving	
73	More Problem Solving	
74	More Problem Solving	

MY INCENTIVE IS ✖

75	Counting Coins	
76	Counting Coins	
77	Dividing Money	
78	Money Practice	
79	Word Problem Solving	

MY INCENTIVE IS ✖

80	Adding Doubles	
81	Addition Problem Solving	
82	Subtraction Problem Solving	
83	Addition: More Problem Solving	
84	Subtraction: More Problem Solving	
85	Column Addition	
86	2-Digit Numeral Addition	
87	2-Digit Numeral Subtraction	

MY INCENTIVE IS ✖

88	Mixed Practice: Two Digit Add/Subtract	
89	Mixed Practice: Addition/Subtraction 0-18	
90	Mixed Practice: Facts 0-18	

MY INCENTIVE IS ✖

Diagnostic Test

Name _____

Directions: Complete the following problems. Follow the directions for a specific problem if they are present. For each question, fill in the circle of the correct answer.

---

1. How many pears are shown below?

- ○ A.   2
- ○ B.   7
- ○ C.   9

2. How many rulers are shown below?

- ○ A. five
- ○ B. three
- ○ C. six

3. How many sheets of paper are shown below?

- ○ A. nine
- ○ B. two
- ○ C. eleven

4. How many diamonds are circled?

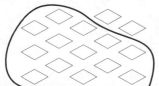

- ○ A.   13
- ○ B.   12
- ○ C.   10

5. Which group has more?

```
  R              Z Z
 R R           Z  Z Z
R R R          Z Z Z
 R  R           Z Z
  R
```

- ○ A.   ○ B.

6. Which group has more?

```
 K K           M M M M
K K K          M M M
 K K           M M M
```

- ○ A.   ○ B.

---

7. What number comes <u>before</u> 12?

- ○ A.   10
- ○ B.   9
- ○ C.   11

8. What number comes <u>between</u> 85 and 87?

- ○ A.   84
- ○ B.   88
- ○ C.   86

9. What number comes <u>after</u> 93?

- ○ A.   92
- ○ B.   90
- ○ C.   94

10. Write the numerals for each number word.

seven   _____

one   _____

twelve   _____

three   _____

11.   2 + 1 =

- ○ A.   3
- ○ B.   4
- ○ C.   1
- ○ D.   5

12. There are 4 fish. 2 more fish come. How many fish are there all together?

    4 + 2 =

- ○ A.   6
- ○ B.   3
- ○ C.   7
- ○ D.   2

Diagnostic Test

Name _____

13. Match the pattern to the correct answer.

◆◆□◆◆

- ○ A. ◆◆□◆◆
- ○ B. ◆◆◆□◆◆◆
- ○ C. ◆◆□□◆◆

14. There were 6 bananas. A monkey ate 2. Now how many bannanas are left?

- ○ A. 8
- ○ B. 4
- ○ C. 5

15.
6
− 2

- ○ A. 4
- ○ B. 2
- ○ C. 3

16.
4
− 4

- ○ A. 0
- ○ B. 4
- ○ C. 1

17. David had 6 candles on his cake. He blew out 3. How many candles are still burning on David's birthday cake?

- ○ A. 1
- ○ B. 3
- ○ C. 2

18.
1
+ 5

- ○ A. 6
- ○ B. 5
- ○ C. 7

19.
6
− 5

- ○ A. 1
- ○ B. 5
- ○ C. 3

20. Which of the following is <u>not</u> part of this number family?

5
3 2

- ○ A. 3 + 2 = 5
- ○ B. 2 + 3 = 5
- ○ C. 5 − 1 = 4
- ○ D. 5 − 3 = 2

21.
6
+ 5

- ○ A. 11
- ○ B. 12
- ○ C. 0

22.
1
+ 6

- ○ A. 7
- ○ B. 5
- ○ C. 8

23. What number comes <u>between</u> 50 and 52?

- ○ A. 49
- ○ B. 51
- ○ C. 53

24. What number comes <u>between</u> 0 and 2?

- ○ A. 5
- ○ B. 1
- ○ C. 3

25.
3
+ 8

- ○ A. 10
- ○ B. 12
- ○ C. 11

26.
4
+ 6

- ○ A. 10
- ○ B. 11
- ○ C. 9

Diagnostic Test

27. David had 12 books. He gave 6 books to Sam. How many does he have left?

○ A. 5   ○ B. 6   ○ C. 4

---

28.   12
        – 0

○ A.   10
○ B.   12
○ C.   11

---

29.   7
        – 1

○ A.   8
○ B.   5
○ C.   6

---

30. How many total sets of ten and how many ones are in this group of coins below?

○ A. 1 ten, 7 ones   ○ B. 2 tens, 5 ones
○ C. 1 ten, 5 ones   ○ D. 3 tens, 0 ones

---

31. How many total sets of ten and how many ones are in this group of circles below?

○ A. 3 tens, 3 ones   ○ B. 3 tens, 4 ones
○ C. 2 tens, 4 ones   ○ D. 3 tens, 5 ones

---

32. How many total sets of ten and how many ones are in this group of sticks below?

○ A. 6 tens, 4 ones   ○ B. 5 tens, 3 ones
○ C. 6 tens, 3 ones   ○ D. 6 tens, 5 ones

---

33. How many total sets of ten and how many ones are in this group of squares below?

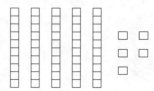

○ A. 5 tens, 5 ones   ○ B. 5 tens, 4 ones
○ C. 6 tens, 6 ones   ○ D. 6 tens, 5 ones

---

34. Which one is greater?

○ A. 6 tens, 9 ones   ○ B. 9 tens, 6 ones

---

35. What time does the face of this clock show?

○ A.   11:00
○ B.   12:00
○ C.   10:00
○ D.   9:00

---

36. Which clock shows the time of 9:00?

○ A.   ○ B.

○ C.    ○ D.

---

37. Which clock shows the time of 3:30?

○ A.   ○ B.

○ C.   ○ D.

Diagnostic Test

Name _____

38. What time does the face of this clock show?

- ○ A. 7:00
- ○ B. 9:00
- ○ C. 8:00
- ○ D. 6:00

39. Which number is greater?

- ○ A. 24
- ○ B. 20

40. Which number is fewer?

- ○ A. 1
- ○ B. 11

41. ___ + 4 = 14

- ○ A. 10
- ○ B. 12
- ○ C. 8
- ○ D. 16

42. 7
     + 4

- ○ A. 11
- ○ B. 10
- ○ C. 12

43. David walked 8 miles on Monday and 7 miles on Tuesday. How far did he walk altogether?

- ○ A. 15
- ○ B. 14
- ○ C. 16

44. 8 fat pigs eating. 5 thin pigs eating. How many pigs are eating?

- ○ A. 15
- ○ B. 13
- ○ C. 16

45. 14
     – 11

- ○ A. 4
- ○ B. 13
- ○ C. 3

46. How many cents?

- ○ A. 50¢
- ○ B. 52¢
- ○ C. 55¢
- ○ D. 42¢

47. How many cents?

- ○ A. 50¢
- ○ B. 56¢
- ○ C. 52¢
- ○ D. 66¢

48. 3
     2
   + 3

- ○ A. 10
- ○ B. 8
- ○ C. 6
- ○ D. 9

49. 13
    + 86

- ○ A. 100
- ○ B. 99
- ○ C. 90

50. 95
     – 23

- ○ A. 72
- ○ B. 70
- ○ C. 62

Check Yourself

Diagnostic Test Analysis

After you review your student's diagnostic test, match those problems that contain incorrect answers to the sections below. Pay special attention to the pages which fall into these problem sections and insure that your student receives supervision in these areas. In this way, your student will strengthen math skills for these sections.

Quantity

Diagnostic Problem Numbers:
1, 2, 3, 4

Review These Pages in Main Book:
11, 12

Intermediate Addition & Subtraction

Diagnostic Problem Numbers:
19, 20, 21, 22, 25, 26, 27, 28, 29

Review These Pages in Main Book:
35, 36, 37, 38, 39, 40, 41, 42, 43, 44, 45

Comparison

Diagnostic Problem Numbers:
5, 6, 13, 34, 39, 40

Review These Pages in Main Book:
14, 50, 59

Place Value

Diagnostic Problem Numbers:
30, 31, 32, 33

Review These Pages in Main Book:
46, 47, 48, 49, 50

Numerals & Number Words

Diagnostic Problem Numbers:
7, 8, 9, 10, 23, 24

Review These Pages in Main Book:
15, 16, 17, 18, 19, 20, 37

Telling Time

Diagnostic Problem Numbers:
35, 36, 37, 38

Review These Pages in Main Book:
51, 52, 53, 54, 55, 56

Simple Addition 0 – 6

Diagnostic Problem Numbers:
11, 12, 18

Review These Pages in Main Book:
20, 21, 22, 23

Complex Addition & Subtraction

Diagnostic Problem Numbers:
41, 42, 43, 44, 45, 48, 49, 50

Review These Pages in Main Book:
63 - 74, 80 - 90

Simple Subtraction 0 – 6

Diagnostic Problem Numbers:
14, 15, 16, 17

Review These Pages in Main Book:
24, 25, 26, 27, 28

Money

Diagnostic Problem Numbers:
46, 47

Review These Pages in Main Book:
75, 76, 78, 79

Number Writing Practice

Practice writing numerals (numbers) 0-10. Write a row of each.

0							
1							
2							
3							
4							
5							
6							
7							
8							
9							
10							

Quantity: Multiple Choice Practice

Circle the numeral that tells how many. The first one is done for you.

1.

(4)   8   6

2.

0   3   10

3.

2   7   9

4.

11   1   5

5.

3   5   12

6.

0   7   9

7.

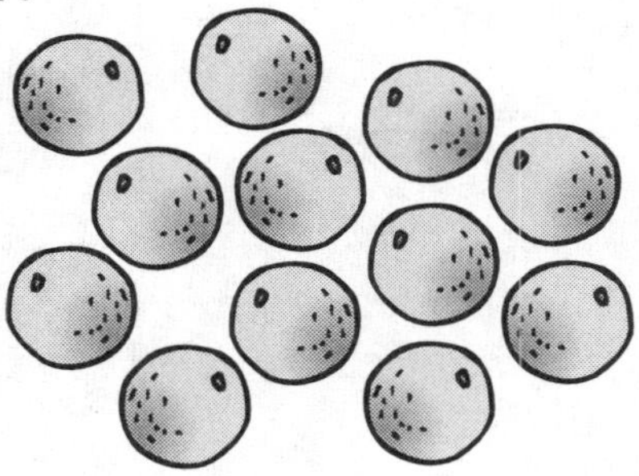

6   12   3

8.

8   1   4

9.

11   10   2

Quantity: Writing Numerals

Write the numeral that tells how many. The first one is done for you.

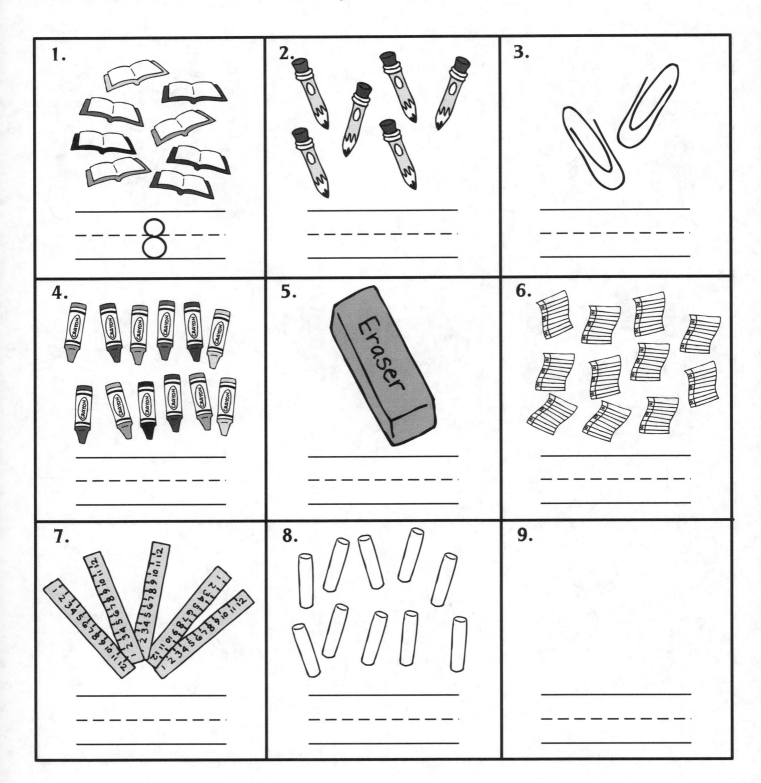

Counting

Touch each numeral, saying it out loud.

1	2	3	4	5	6	7	8	9	10
11	12	13	14	15	16	17	18	19	20

Write the missing numerals.

1		3						9	
				15					20

Write the numerals 1-20.

Draw and color 20 objects of your choice.

Comparison: Greater vs. Fewer

Count the letters, write how many, then circle the one that is greater.

1. Example:

A A   T T
A A A   T
A A A   T T
A   T

(9)   6
___   ___

2.

S S   Y
S S S   Y Y
S S S   Y Y Y
S S S   Y Y Y
   Y

___   ___

3.

R   Z Z
R R   Z Z
R R   Z Z
R R   Z Z

___   ___

Count the letters, write how many, then circle the one that is fewer.

4. Example:

G   I I
G G   I I
G G   I
G G   I

7   (5)
___   ___

5.

K   M M
K K   M M
K K   M M
K K   M M
K   M M

___   ___

6.

O O   P P
O O O   P P
O O   P P
O O O   P P
O O   P

___   ___

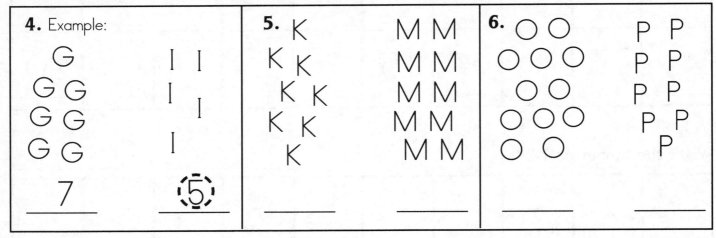

Draw two fewer circles than those shown below.

7. ◯ ◯ ◯ ◯ ◯ ◯ ◯ ◯ ◯

Circle the numerals that are fewer than 10.

6   12   8   4   0   19   16   18   2   9   20   1

Writing Numerals: 1 to 100

Write the numerals to 100. Start with 4.

1	2	3							

Before, After, Between. Write the numeral that comes before, between or after each numeral listed below. The first row is done for you.

Before		Between			After	
9	10	0	1	2	89	90
___	6	25	___	27	17	___
___	12	71	___	73	29	___
___	21	19	___	21	80	___
___	38	85	___	87	19	___
___	14	49	___	51	77	___
___	3	93	___	95	39	___
___	67	99	___	101	93	___
___	49	13	___	15	21	___
___	8	58	___	60	66	___
___	100	10	___	12	15	___

Number Words

The following numerals and number words go together:

0–zero	1–one	2–two	3–three	4–four
5–five	6–six	7–seven	8–eight	9–nine
10–ten	11–eleven	12–twelve		

Write the number word by each numeral. The first one is done for you.

5 _____five_____	4 _____	12 _____
8 _____	7 _____	2 _____
0 _____	9 _____	10 _____
3 _____	1 _____	11 _____
6 _____		

Write the number word to tell how many. The first one is done for you.

1.  _____eight_____

2.    _____

3. 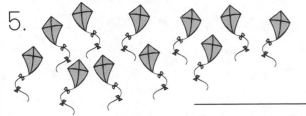 _____

4.   _____

5.   _____

6. 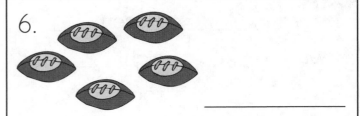 _____

Number Word Search

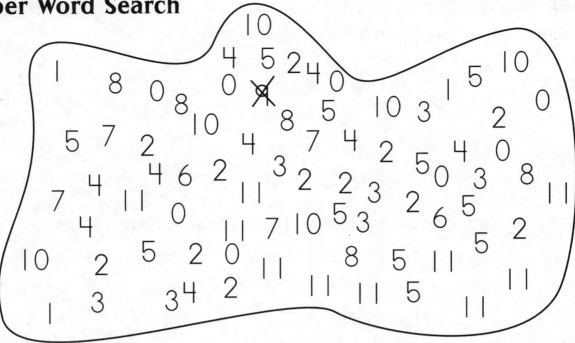

Count the number of times each numeral from 0-12 appears in the balloon. Then write your answer, as a number word, next to the letter which contains the correct amount of times that each numeral appears. Cross out numerals as you count to make the exercise easier. The first numeral is done for you.

A.	1	_____nine_____	
B.	2	_____	
C.	3	_____	
D.	4	_____	
E.	5	_____	
F.	6	_____	
G.	7	_____	

H.	8	_____
I.	9	_____
J.	10	_____
K.	11	_____
L.	12	_____
M.	0	_____

 Write the numerals. The first one is done for you.

						zero	_0_
seven	___	eleven	___	five	___	twelve	___
two	___	eight	___	one	___	ten	___
six	___	four	___	three	___	nine	___

Number Word Application

0–zero	1–one	2–two	3–three	4–four
5–five	6–six	7–seven	8–eight	9–nine
10–ten	11–eleven	12–twelve		

Use the number words at the top of the page to help answer the following questions. Fill in each blank with a number word, not a numeral. The first one is done for you.

1. Three comes after _____two_____.

2. Seven is one less than _____.

3. Two comes between _____ and _____.

4. Twelve is one more than _____.

5. Zero comes before _____.

6. Eight comes between _____ and _____.

7. Three comes between _____ and _____.

8. Nine comes after _____.

9. Five is two more than _____.

10. Ten comes before _____.

11. One is one less than _____.

12. Four is one more than _____.

13. Six comes between _____ and _____.

14. Eleven is two more than _____.

15. Seven is one more than _____.

16. Ten is two less than _____.

17. Nine comes between _____ and _____.

18. Eight is two more than _____.

19. Zero is four less than _____.

20. Two is two more than _____.

Addition 0 — 6: Problem Solving

Read each problem, follow the coloring instructions, solve the problem and then write the number word on the line and the numeral in the box. The first one is done for you.

1. Can you see 5 carrots?

Color 2 green.

Color 3 orange.

2 green and 3 orange make _____ five _____.

$$\begin{array}{r} 2 \\ + 3 \\ \hline \boxed{5} \end{array}$$

green   orange

2. Can you see 4 buttons?

Color 1 blue.

Color 3 red.

1 blue and 3 red make _____.

$$\begin{array}{r} 1 \\ + 3 \\ \hline \boxed{} \end{array}$$

3. Now look at these apples.

Color 4 red.

Color 2 yellow.

4 red and 2 yellow make _____.

$$\begin{array}{r} 4 \\ + 2 \\ \hline \boxed{} \end{array}$$

4. Count these stars

Color 2 stars yellow.

Color 0 stars blue.

2 yellow stars and 0 blue stars

make _____.

$$\begin{array}{r} 2 \\ + 0 \\ \hline \boxed{} \end{array}$$

Solve each problem. The first one is done for you.

3 + 1 = ___4___   1 + 1 = _____   3 + 3 = _____

2 + 4 = _____   2 + 2 = _____   0 + 6 = _____

0 + 2 = _____   5 + 0 = _____   1 + 5 = _____

3 + 2 = _____   4 + 1 = _____   1 + 2 = _____

Addition 0 — 6: Problem Solving

Solve each problem below. The first one is done for you.

1.

4 + 1 = ____5____

2.

3 + 2 = _____

3.

3 + _____ = _____

4.

_____ + 0 = _____

5.

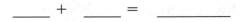 ____ + ____ = _____

6.

____ + ____ = _____

 **Solve each problem. The first one is done for you.**

1 + __1__ = 2   _____ + 3 = 5   4 + ____ = 4

3 + ____ = 6   _____ + 0 = 4   _____ + 2 = 3

2 + ____ = 4   _____ + 1 = 3   _____ + 3 = 3

5 + ____ = 6   _____ + 0 = 0   1 + ____ = 5

Addition 0 — 6: Mixed Equation Practice

Solve each problem below. The first one in each section is done for you.

1. 2 + 1 = ___3___   3 + 2 = _____   1 + 1 = _____

2. 0 + 6 = _____   4 + 1 = _____   0 + 0 = _____

3. 1 + 3 = _____   3 + 3 = _____   5 + 1 = _____

4.
$$\begin{array}{r} 0 \\ +1 \\ \hline 1 \end{array} \qquad \begin{array}{r} 2 \\ +3 \\ \hline \end{array} \qquad \begin{array}{r} 2 \\ +2 \\ \hline \end{array} \qquad \begin{array}{r} 2 \\ +0 \\ \hline \end{array} \qquad \begin{array}{r} 1 \\ +5 \\ \hline \end{array}$$

5.
$$\begin{array}{r} 2 \\ +4 \\ \hline \end{array} \qquad \begin{array}{r} 4 \\ +0 \\ \hline \end{array} \qquad \begin{array}{r} 0 \\ +4 \\ \hline \end{array} \qquad \begin{array}{r} 1 \\ +2 \\ \hline \end{array} \qquad \begin{array}{r} 0 \\ +5 \\ \hline \end{array}$$

6.
$$\begin{array}{r} 0 \\ +2 \\ \hline \end{array} \qquad \begin{array}{r} 1 \\ +4 \\ \hline \end{array} \qquad \begin{array}{r} 4 \\ +2 \\ \hline \end{array} \qquad \begin{array}{r} 3 \\ +0 \\ \hline \end{array} \qquad \begin{array}{r} 2 \\ +4 \\ \hline \end{array}$$

7.
$$\begin{array}{r} 1 \\ +0 \\ \hline \end{array} \qquad \begin{array}{r} 5 \\ +0 \\ \hline \end{array} \qquad \begin{array}{r} 0 \\ +3 \\ \hline \end{array} \qquad \begin{array}{r} 3 \\ +1 \\ \hline \end{array} \qquad \begin{array}{r} 0 \\ +6 \\ \hline \end{array}$$

Write the sum for each equation. Then underline the two problems in each numbered exercise which have the same sum. The first one is done for you.

8. <u>4 + 2 = ___6___</u>   <u>3 + 3 = ___6___</u>   1 + 2 = ___3___

9. 1 + 1 = _____   3 + 1 = _____   2 + 0 = _____

10. 3 + 2 = _____   1 + 4 = _____   1 + 5 = _____

11. 1 + 4 = _____   1 + 2 = _____   3 + 0 = _____

12. 2 + 2 = _____   0 + 6 = _____   1 + 3 = _____

Name _____

Word Problem Solving. Read the story and solve the problem.
Write the problem out in the box or on the lines. The first one is done for you.

---

1. There are 3 red pencils.
There are 2 blue ones.
How may pencils are
there in all?
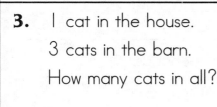

$$\begin{array}{r} 3 \\ +\ 2 \\ \hline 5 \end{array}$$

2. There were 4 fish.
2 more fish came.
How many fish were there
altogether?
4 + 2 = _____
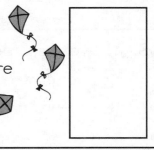

---

3. I cat in the house.
3 cats in the barn.
How many cats in all?

____ + ____ = _____

4. There are 2 kites.
I more blows in.
How many kites are
in the sky?
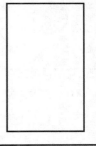

---

5. She had 4 apples.
He had none.
How many apples did
they have?
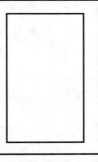

6. There are 5 baseballs.
There is 1 bat.
How many balls and bats
are there altogether?

---

7. 3 buttons on a string.
Ann put 3 more buttons on.
Now there are _____ buttons
on the string.

____ + ____ = _____

8. There were 0 eggs in the nest.
A bird lays 3 eggs in the nest.
How many total eggs were
in the nest?

____ + ____ = _____

---

9. I worm was out.
4 more came out.
How many worms came
out altogether?

10. Ann has 6 pencils.
Sam has 0 pencils.
How many pencils do the
2 children have?

Subtraction 0 — 6: Problem Solving

Read the story and write the difference. The first one is done for you.

1. There are 2 sail boats.

I floats away.

How many are left?

2 – 1 = ___1___

2. There are 5 birds.

I flies away.

How many are left?

5 – 1 = _____

3. There are 3 pennies.

2 pennies were lost.

How many are left?

$\begin{array}{r} 3 \\ -\,2 \\ \hline \end{array}$

4. There are 6 bananas.

A monkey ate 2.

Now how many bananas are there?

$\begin{array}{r} 6 \\ -\,2 \\ \hline \end{array}$

5. There are 6 zero's.

O O O O O O

Cross out 4.

How many are not crossed out?

6 – 4 = _____

6. There are 4 fish in a tank.

No fish left.

How many fish are in the tank?

4 – 0 = _____

7. There are 6 rabbits.

I hops away.

How many are left?

$\begin{array}{r} 6 \\ -\,1 \\ \hline \end{array}$

8. There are 5 flowers.

2 get stepped on.

How many are left?

5 – 2 = _____

Subtraction 0 — 6: Writing Equations

Write a math sentence to go with each picture. The first one is done for you.

1.  3 - __1__ = __2__	**2.**  2 - ___ = ___
3. 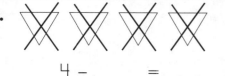 4 - ___ = ___	**4.** 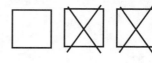 ___ - ___ = ___
5. 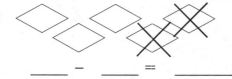 ___ - ___ = ___	**6.** 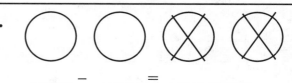 ___ - ___ = ___
7. 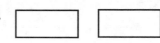 ___ - ___ = ___	**8.** 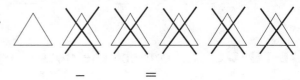 ___ - ___ = ___
9. ___ - ___ = ___	**10.** ___ - ___ = ___

Keeping Up

Fill in the blanks to complete each numerical sequence.

1. 10 ___ 12 ___ ___ ___ 16 ___ ___

2. ___ ___ ___ 16 ___ ___ 19 ___

Subtraction 0 — 6: Mixed Equation Practice. Find each difference.

Example:

1. 1 – 0 = ___1___   2 – 0 = _____   4 – 0 = _____

2. 5 – 5 = _____   1 – 1 = _____   2 – 2 = _____

3. 6 – 4 = _____   5 – 2 = _____   3 – 1 = _____

4. 2 – 1 = _____   6 – 6 = _____   4 – 3 = _____

Example:

5.
$$6 \atop -2$$ 4 $$3 \atop -2$$ $$5 \atop -5$$ $$6 \atop -5$$ $$5 \atop -3$$ $$3 \atop -2$$

6.
$$3 \atop -3$$ $$4 \atop -1$$ $$6 \atop -2$$ $$5 \atop -4$$ $$4 \atop -4$$ $$6 \atop -4$$

7.
$$6 \atop -0$$ $$5 \atop -3$$ $$1 \atop -1$$ $$5 \atop -1$$ $$3 \atop -0$$ $$2 \atop -0$$

8.
$$5 \atop -3$$ $$6 \atop -1$$ $$5 \atop -0$$ $$6 \atop -3$$ $$4 \atop -2$$ $$5 \atop -3$$

Dot-to-Dot. Connect the dots starting at 10, and finishing at 20.

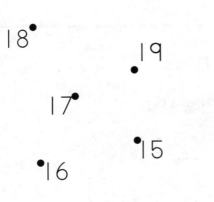

Subtraction 0 — 6: Subtraction Tables

Complete each table. The first problem in each table is done for you.

6	-
0	6
4	
6	
3	
1	
5	
2	

5	-
4	1
2	
0	
5	
1	
3	

4	-
2	2
4	
1	
3	
0	

1	-
0	1
1	

2	-
2	0
1	
0	

3	-
1	2
3	
0	
2	

There are 6 frogs in a pond. 2 frogs left. How many frogs are still in the pond? _____ - _____ = _____

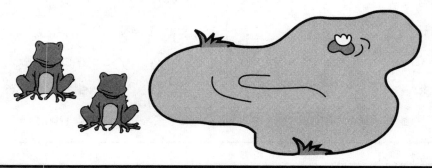

Name _____

Word Problem Solving. Read the story and answer the question.
Write the problem out in the box or on the lines. The first one is done for you.

1. Tom has 2 worms for fishing. 1 worm got out of the can. How many worms are left? 2 - 1 = ___1___	**2.** Jane had 4 dolls. 2 broke. How many does she have left? 4 - 2
3. 5 lights were on in the house. 3 lights were turned off. How many are still on? 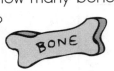	**4.** 6 stars were shining. A cloud covered 4 of them. How many stars are still shinning? ___ - ___ = ___
5. The dog had 6 bones. He did not eat any of them. How many bones does the dog have?  ___ - ___ = ___	**6.** Debra put 5 pennies in her bank. She took out 2 to buy a gum ball. How many pennies are in the bank now? ___ - ___ = ___
7. David had 6 candles on his cake. He blew out 3. How many candles are still burning on David's birthday cake? 	**8.** 3 seals were playing by the pool. 2 seals jumped into the pool. How many seals are left playing by the pool? 

Add or Subtract

Look at the signs and solve each problem. The first one is done for you.

1.

4	0	1	2	0	3
+ 0	+ 6	+ 2	+ 4	+ 5	+ 1
4					

2.

5	4	2	6	5	4
− 3	− 4	− 1	− 3	− 1	− 2

3.

2	0	2	5	1	6
+ 3	+ 4	− 0	− 5	+ 4	− 4

4.

6	4	3	6	4	3
− 6	+ 1	+ 2	− 1	− 0	+ 3

5.

2	0	2	0	6	3
+ 0	− 0	+ 2	+ 1	− 2	− 3

6.

4	0	4	3	3	1
+ 2	+ 2	− 1	− 2	+ 0	+ 1

7.

5	1	5	1	6	6
− 2	+ 3	− 4	+ 5	− 5	+ 0

Addition and Subtraction Trails. Complete each equation string.

1.

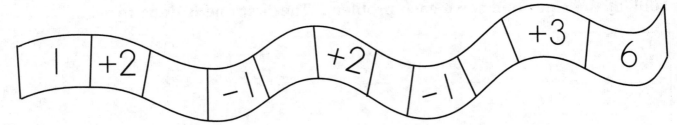

2.

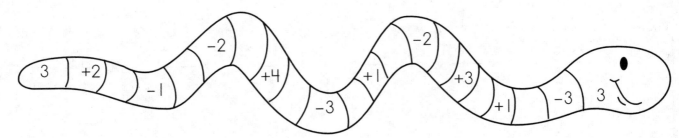

3.

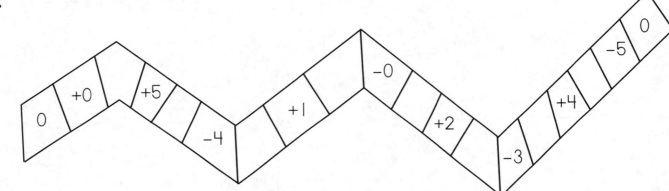

4.

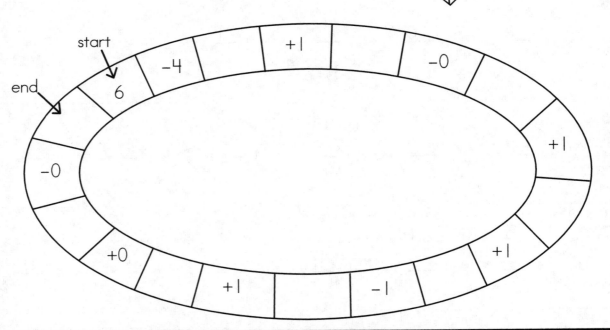

Number Families

Complete each equation below. The first one is done for you.

1.

$$\underline{1} + \underline{3} = \underline{4}$$
$$\underline{3} + \underline{1} = \underline{4}$$
$$\underline{4} - \underline{3} = \underline{1}$$
$$\underline{4} - \underline{1} = \underline{3}$$

2.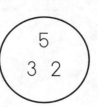

$$\underline{} + \underline{} = \underline{}$$
$$\underline{} + \underline{} = \underline{}$$
$$\underline{} - \underline{} = \underline{}$$
$$\underline{} - \underline{} = \underline{}$$

3.

$$\underline{} + \underline{} = \underline{}$$
$$\underline{} + \underline{} = \underline{}$$
$$\underline{} - \underline{} = \underline{}$$
$$\underline{} - \underline{} = \underline{}$$

4.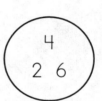

$$\underline{} + \underline{} = \underline{}$$
$$\underline{} + \underline{} = \underline{}$$
$$\underline{} - \underline{} = \underline{}$$
$$\underline{} - \underline{} = \underline{}$$

 **Which numerals are listed only one time in each set below? Circle them.**

1.

3	7	1	12	9	3
9	2	4	6	4	2
8	0	1	2	2	10
11	1	5	8	5	1
2	4	10	0	11	7

2.

20	1	20	5	17	14
3	7	1	6	15	9
17	16	12	2	12	5
2	8	11	15	6	8
9	20	14	16	3	10

Number Words

Count the nuts. Draw a line from the numeral answer that tells how many nuts are shown to the matching number word. The first one is done for you.

1.

2	two
3	five
4	four
5	three

2.

5	ten
8	five
10	seven
7	eight

3.

0	two
3	one
1	three
2	zero

4.

2	ten
9	eight
8	nine
10	two

5.

3	two
2	twelve
12	ten
10	three

6.

8	one
9	seven
7	eight
1	nine

Number Words: Mixed Practice

Count the dots then draw a line from the numeral answer that tells how many dots to the matching number word. The first one is done for you.

1.		2.		3.	
4	eight	one	0	nine	8
8	one	eleven	10	eight	11
5	four	zero	1	six	9
1	five	ten	11	eleven	6

4.		5.		6.	
7	ten	11	eight	4	seven
10	seven	4	eleven	5	six
1	one	2	four	7	five
5	five	8	two	6	four

7.		8.		9.	
11	seven	5	twelve	3	twelve
6	six	12	five	2	three
1	eleven	4	six	10	ten
7	one	6	four	12	two

Write the numeral for each of the number words below. The first one is done for you.

1. seventeen _____17_____   5. eighteen _____

2. twenty _____   6. fifteen _____

3. fourteen _____   7. nineteen _____

4. sixteen _____   8. thirteen _____

Bar Graph

This graph shows which colors Miss George's art class liked best. Use the graph to answer the questions below and fill in the blanks. The first one is done for you.

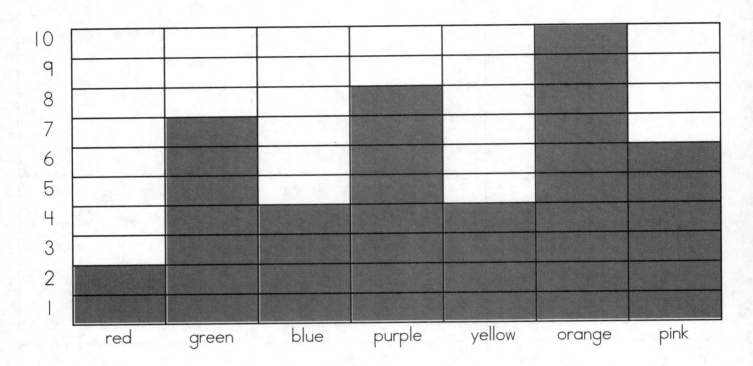

1. The greater number of children liked _____orange_____ best.

2. The least favorite color was _____.

3. How many children choose green? _____

4. Which two colors have the same amount? _____, _____

5. How many more children choose orange over green? _____

6. How many children liked pink best? _____

7. Write a number sentence to show how many liked blue and red. _____

8. Write a number sentence to show how many less children like yellow instead of pink. _____

9. Color in a box to show which color you like best.

10. How many children are in Miss George's art class? _____

Addition 7—12: Problem Solving

Count the objects to help you find the sums. The first one is done for you.

1.

$2 + 5 =$ ___7___

2.

$4 + 5 =$ _____

3.

$8 + 3 =$ _____

4.

$7 + 0 =$ _____

5.

$6 + 4 =$ _____

6.

$1 + 8 =$ _____

7.

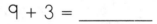

$9 + 3 =$ _____

8.

$5 + 5 =$ _____

9.

$3 + 4 =$ _____

10.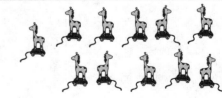

$0 + 11 =$ _____

Addition 7—12: Matching Equations and Answers

Draw a line to the answer that solves each problem. The first one is done for you.

1.		2.		3.	
6 + 2 =	11	5 + 2 =	10	8 + 0 =	11
7 + 4 =	10	6 + 3 =	8	4 + 6 =	9
8 + 1 =	12	2 + 9 =	12	1 + 11 =	7
1 + 6 =	8	3 + 9 =	11	0 + 9 =	12
5 + 5 =	7	4 + 4 =	9	6 + 1 =	8
4 + 8 =	9	8 + 2 =	7	9 + 2 =	10

4.		5.		6.	
1 + 10 =	12	11 + 1 =	9	7 + 3 =	8
8 + 4 =	8	9 + 0 =	7	3 + 8 =	9
7 + 2 =	7	6 + 5 =	12	1 + 7 =	10
6 + 2 =	11	5 + 3 =	10	12 + 0 =	11
0 + 10 =	10	1 + 6 =	11	0 + 7 =	12
4 + 3 =	9	2 + 8 =	8	5 + 4 =	7

7.		8.		9.	
5 + 6 =	9	1 + 9 =	10	0 + 12 =	8
2 + 5 =	8	2 + 6 =	8	2 + 8 =	10
8 + 2 =	11	6 + 6 =	12	3 + 5 =	9
10 + 2 =	7	2 + 7 =	9	11 + 0 =	12
0 + 8 =	12	4 + 7 =	11	4 + 3 =	11
3 + 6 =	10	3 + 4 =	7	3 + 6 =	7

10.		11.		12.	
2 + 10 =	10	7 + 5 =	11	7 + 2 =	8
3 + 7 =	12	9 + 1 =	12	5 + 7 =	10
7 + 1 =	11	10 + 1 =	10	6 + 5 =	11
2 + 9 =	8	3 + 5 =	8	10 + 0 =	12
3 + 6 =	9	6 + 3 =	9	2 + 6 =	9

Addition 7—12: Word Problem Solving

Read the stories and write a number sentence or problem to tell the answer.
The first one is done for you.

---

1. Mother hen has 4 chicks. Mother pig has 5 piglets. How many babies do they have in all?

$$\underline{\quad4\quad} + \underline{\quad5\quad} = \underline{\quad9\quad}$$

2. Jim has 8 toy cars. He got 2 more for his birthday. How many cars does he have?

$$\underline{\qquad} + \underline{\qquad} = \underline{\qquad\qquad}$$

---

3. Sue bought 3 candy bars. Her mother gave her 8 more for her friends. How many does she have?

$$\underline{\qquad} + \underline{\qquad} = \underline{\qquad}$$

4. Amanda read 1 book today and 7 last week. How many books has she read?

---

5. Farmer Fisher had 6 brown and 6 black cows. How many cows did he have in all?

6. Mark has 5 sisters and 2 brothers. How many brothers and sisters does Mark have altogether?

Keeping Up

Write the numeral that comes between. The first one is done for you.

24 __25__ 26   19 _____ 21   98 _____ 100

48 _____ 50   66 _____ 68   81 _____ 83

77 _____ 79   50 _____ 52   59 _____ 61

14 _____ 16   39 _____ 41   10 _____ 12

21 _____ 23   0 _____ 2   33 _____ 35

Name _____

Addition 7—12: Intensive Practice. The first one is done for you.

1.
$$\begin{array}{r} 4 \\ +7 \\ \hline 11 \end{array}$$
$$\begin{array}{r} 3 \\ +9 \\ \hline \end{array}$$
$$\begin{array}{r} 8 \\ +3 \\ \hline \end{array}$$
$$\begin{array}{r} 12 \\ +0 \\ \hline \end{array}$$
$$\begin{array}{r} 0 \\ +10 \\ \hline \end{array}$$
$$\begin{array}{r} 7 \\ +4 \\ \hline \end{array}$$

2.
$$\begin{array}{r} 1 \\ +6 \\ \hline \end{array}$$
$$\begin{array}{r} 2 \\ +5 \\ \hline \end{array}$$
$$\begin{array}{r} 3 \\ +5 \\ \hline \end{array}$$
$$\begin{array}{r} 4 \\ +4 \\ \hline \end{array}$$
$$\begin{array}{r} 9 \\ +0 \\ \hline \end{array}$$
$$\begin{array}{r} 7 \\ +2 \\ \hline \end{array}$$

3.
$$\begin{array}{r} 6 \\ +5 \\ \hline \end{array}$$
$$\begin{array}{r} 7 \\ +5 \\ \hline \end{array}$$
$$\begin{array}{r} 11 \\ +0 \\ \hline \end{array}$$
$$\begin{array}{r} 6 \\ +2 \\ \hline \end{array}$$
$$\begin{array}{r} 2 \\ +8 \\ \hline \end{array}$$
$$\begin{array}{r} 0 \\ +12 \\ \hline \end{array}$$

4.
$$\begin{array}{r} 2 \\ +7 \\ \hline \end{array}$$
$$\begin{array}{r} 4 \\ +5 \\ \hline \end{array}$$
$$\begin{array}{r} 8 \\ +1 \\ \hline \end{array}$$
$$\begin{array}{r} 5 \\ +5 \\ \hline \end{array}$$
$$\begin{array}{r} 10 \\ +2 \\ \hline \end{array}$$
$$\begin{array}{r} 2 \\ +9 \\ \hline \end{array}$$

5.
$$\begin{array}{r} 6 \\ +6 \\ \hline \end{array}$$
$$\begin{array}{r} 2 \\ +10 \\ \hline \end{array}$$
$$\begin{array}{r} 3 \\ +8 \\ \hline \end{array}$$
$$\begin{array}{r} 9 \\ +2 \\ \hline \end{array}$$
$$\begin{array}{r} 4 \\ +6 \\ \hline \end{array}$$
$$\begin{array}{r} 1 \\ +10 \\ \hline \end{array}$$

6.
$$\begin{array}{r} 1 \\ +8 \\ \hline \end{array}$$
$$\begin{array}{r} 0 \\ +7 \\ \hline \end{array}$$
$$\begin{array}{r} 4 \\ +7 \\ \hline \end{array}$$
$$\begin{array}{r} 9 \\ +1 \\ \hline \end{array}$$
$$\begin{array}{r} 5 \\ +6 \\ \hline \end{array}$$
$$\begin{array}{r} 1 \\ +7 \\ \hline \end{array}$$

Odd or Even Numbers
Circle the odd numbers and cross out the even ones.

1 2 3 4 5 6 7 8 9 10 11 12

Name _____

Addition 7—12: Write the Sums. Color the spaces with answers of
7 blue, 8 purple, 9 yellow, 10 orange, 11 green, and 12 pink.

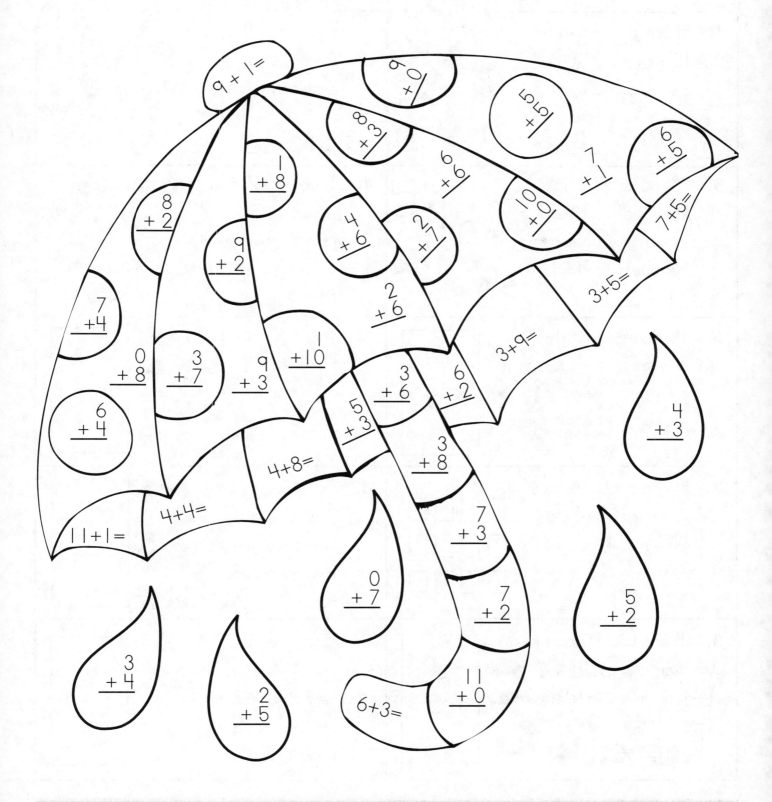

Name _____

Subtraction 7—12: Problem Solving

Count back to help you find the difference. The first one is done for you.

1. There are 7 pennies.
4 roll away.
How many are left?

7 – 4 = ___3___

2. There are 9 lollipops.
2 were eaten.
How many are left?

9 – 2 = _____

3. Mike has 11 books.
He read 5 books.
How many does he
have left to read?

11 – ___ = ___

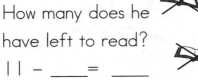

4. There are 8 fish.
3 swam away.
How many are left?

8 – ___ = ___

5. There were 10 shells.
5 were broken.
How many were
broken?

10
– 5
———

6. There are 12 balls.
Cross off 6.
How many
are left?

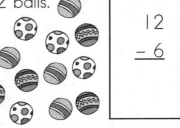

12
– 6
———

7. There are 12 boxes.
Cross off 4.
How many are not
crossed off?

12 – ☐ = ___

8. There are 11 cups.
7 were used for
hot chocolate.
How many were
not used?

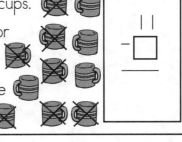

11
– ☐
———

9. There are 10 doughnuts
Dan ate 6.
How many are left?

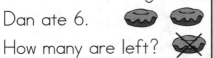

10
– ☐
———

10. There are 12
eggs. Mom
used 2 for the
cake. How many
eggs are left?

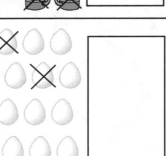

Subtraction 7—12: Matching Equations and Answers

Draw a line to the correct answer. The first one is done for you.

1.		**2.**		**3.**	
9 – 1 =	7	10 – 0 =	0	11 – 4 =	3
10 – 3 =	8	7 – 7 =	5	8 – 4 =	10
11 – 9 =	0	11 – 8 =	10	12 – 9 =	7
7 – 4 =	3	9 – 3 =	8	7 – 6 =	1
8 – 7 =	2	10 – 5 =	6	11 – 1 =	5
12 – 12 =	1	12 – 4 =	3	9 – 4 =	4

4.		**5.**		**6.**	
12 – 8 =	2	9 – 9 =	7	10 – 9 =	2
12 – 6 =	3	11 – 6 =	4	8 – 6 =	1
10 – 8 =	4	7 – 0 =	0	12 – 0 =	4
11 – 11 =	0	12 – 10 =	1	11 – 7 =	12
10 – 7 =	5	9 – 8 =	2	12 – 11 =	4
8 – 3 =	6	7 – 3 =	5	9 – 5 =	1

7.		**8.**		**9.**	
12 – 1 =	9	9 – 6 =	3	7 – 2 =	8
11 – 2 =	5	10 – 2 =	8	10 – 10 =	5
8 – 1 =	1	11 – 0 =	11	12 – 3 =	0
7 – 6 =	11	12 – 2 =	10	9 – 7 =	9
12 – 7 =	4	11 – 10 =	1	11 – 1 =	2
10 – 6 =	7	8 – 5 =	3	8 – 0 =	10

10.		**11.**		**12.**	
7 – 5 =	8	8 – 2 =	10	10 – 4 =	6
9 – 5 =	2	12 – 2 =	5	10 – 6 =	3
8 – 0 =	9	11 – 6 =	6	8 – 5 =	9
10 – 1 =	4	12 – 4 =	0	9 – 0 =	5
11 – 3 =	8	8 – 8 =	8	9 – 4 =	4

Name _____

Subtraction 7—12: Multiple Choice Problem Solving

Fill in the box by the correct answer. The first one is done for you.

1. $9 - 2 =$ 2 ☐ 9 ☐ 7 ■	2. $10 - 7 =$ 3 ☐ 4 ☐ 5 ☐	3. $7 - 5 =$ 6 ☐ 12 ☐ 2 ☐
4. $12 - 5 =$ 8 ☐ 7 ☐ 4 ☐	5. $11 - 9 =$ 2 ☐ 9 ☐ 3 ☐	6. $8 - 6 =$ 4 ☐ 3 ☐ 2 ☐
7. $12 - 3 =$ 9 ☐ 8 ☐ 6 ☐	8. $9 - 7 =$ 6 ☐ 4 ☐ 2 ☐	9. $11 - 2 =$ 6 ☐ 9 ☐ 3 ☐
10. $7 - 4 =$ 3 ☐ 2 ☐ 1 ☐	11. $8 - 5 =$ 3 ☐ 5 ☐ 9 ☐	12. $12 - 8 =$ 6 ☐ 5 ☐ 4 ☐
13. $10 - 0$ 12 ☐ 4 ☐ 10 ☐	14. $10 - 10 =$ 10 ☐ 9 ☐ 0 ☐	15. $9 - 6 =$ 3 ☐ 4 ☐ 5 ☐
16. $12 - 9 =$ 9 ☐ 6 ☐ 3 ☐	17. $11 - 4 =$ 6 ☐ 7 ☐ 8 ☐	18. $8 - 2 =$ 6 ☐ 8 ☐ 5 ☐
19. $12 - 12 =$ 0 ☐ 2 ☐ 4 ☐ 6 ☐	20. $7 - 6 =$ 1 ☐ 2 ☐ 3 ☐ 0 ☐	21. $11 - 6 =$ 6 ☐ 4 ☐ 5 ☐ 9 ☐

Subtraction 7—12: Comparison

Complete the problems then circle those which equal the numeral in the box.
The first two are done for you.

1.

$(10 - 2 = 8)$
$10 - 1 = 9$
$11 - 3 =$
$11 - 0 =$
$12 - 4 =$
$8 - 0 =$

2. 9

$7 - 2 =$
$12 - 3 =$
$10 - 1 =$
$11 - 2 =$
$10 - 8 =$
$9 - 0 =$

3. 7

$8 - 1 =$
$9 - 2 =$
$10 - 5 =$
$7 - 4 =$
$11 - 4 =$
$12 - 5 =$

4. 12

$12 - 1 =$
$12 - 6 =$
$11 - 2 =$
$12 - 0 =$

5. 10

$11 - 1 =$
$10 - 10 =$
$10 - 0 =$
$12 - 2 =$

6. 11

$11 - 6 =$
$12 - 1 =$
$11 - 0 =$
$12 - 9 =$

7. 6

$8 - 2 =$
$9 - 5 =$
$10 - 4 =$
$12 - 7 =$
$11 - 5 =$
$12 - 10 =$

8. 4

$2 - 2 =$
$9 - 5 =$
$11 - 7 =$
$8 - 2 =$
$10 - 6 =$
$12 - 8 =$

9. 5

$11 - 6 =$
$9 - 4 =$
$7 - 2 =$
$10 - 3 =$
$8 - 3 =$
$12 - 7 =$

Keeping Up. Write the numeral. The first one is done for you.

twelve __12__   nine _____   eleven _____   one _____

four _____   seven _____   eight _____   five _____

Subtraction 7 —12: Word Problem Solving

Read the story. Write the greater numeral from the story first, in a math sentence, to solve the problem.

1. Mark has 12 pears in a basket. 4 of the pears were ripe. How many were not ripe?

   $\underline{12} - \underline{4} = \underline{8}$

2. Julie had 7 marbles in a bag. She lost 5 because the bag had a hole in it. How many marbles does she have?

   _____ - _____ = _____

3. Jim had 9 cookies in his lunch box. He gave 4 to his dad. How many cookies did Jim have left?

   _____ - _____ = _____

4. David had 12 books. He gave 6 books to Sam. How many did he have left?

   _____ - _____ = _____

5. 11 children were swimming. 8 were boys. How many were girls?

   _____ - _____ = _____

6. There were 8 trees in my yard. I had 2 cut down. How many trees do I have left?

   _____ - _____ = _____

7. Mr. Hobbs had 10 rows of carrots in his garden. 3 rows did not grow. How many rows did grow?

   _____ - _____ = _____

8. Ann had 12 flowers. 9 were yellow and the rest were red. How many were red?

   _____ - _____ = _____

Name _____

Subtraction 7—12: Intensive Practice. The first one is done for you.

1.

8	9	12	10	7	11
− 4	− 1	− 12	− 2	− 4	− 5
4					

2.

12	9	11	7	12	10
− 6	− 7	− 7	− 7	− 3	− 10

3.

11	8	7	12	10	11
− 6	− 3	− 0	− 7	− 5	− 9

4.

10	7	11	12	8	12
− 6	− 6	− 0	− 10	− 6	− 8

5.

8	12	11	9	7	12
− 5	− 0	− 2	− 3	− 1	− 5

6.

9	11	7	12	10	8
− 5	− 4	− 2	− 1	− 8	− 1

 There are 12 total eggs. The eggs shown below are outside of the nest. How many eggs are in the nest?

        _____

Place Value: Tens and Ones

Circle ten pennies in each row. Write down how many you did not circle.
The first one is done for you.

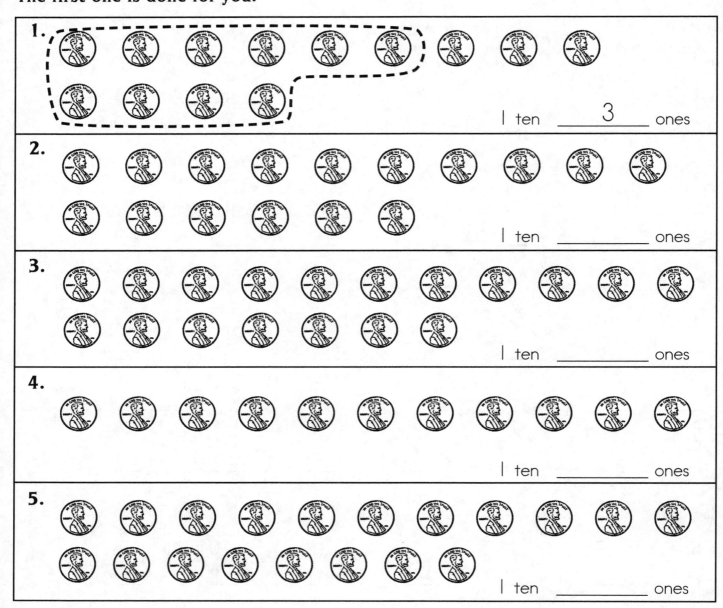

1. I ten ___3___ ones

2. I ten _____ ones

3. I ten _____ ones

4. I ten _____ ones

5. I ten _____ ones

Keeping Up. Write the numeral that is the same as the number word.

The first one is done for you.

two ___2___   three _____   ten _____   twelve _____

six _____   nine _____   zero _____   eight _____

Place Value: Tens and Ones.

Circle 10 pennies. Write how many sets of ten and how many ones are in each problem. The first one is done for you.

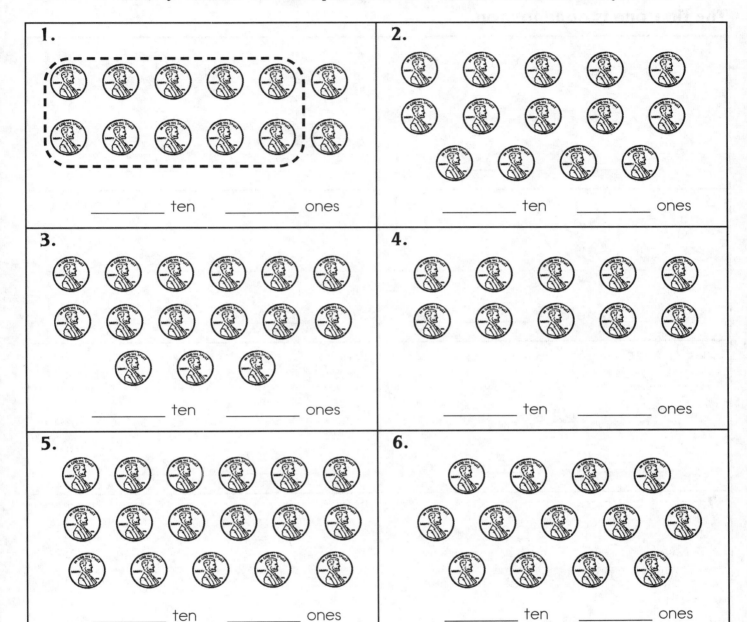

1.

_____ ten   _____ ones

2.

_____ ten   _____ ones

3.

_____ ten   _____ ones

4.

_____ ten   _____ ones

5.

_____ ten   _____ ones

6.

_____ ten   _____ ones

Keeping Up. Write the numeral that comes before each one listed.

Example: __41__ 42   _____ 10   _____ 96   _____ 31

_____ 38   _____ 20   _____ 40   _____ 18

_____ 14   _____ 66   _____ 16   _____ 90

_____ 80   _____ 7

Place Value: Tens and Ones

Write how many sets of ten and how many ones are in each problem.
The first one is done for you.

1. _____1_____ ten _____3_____ ones	**2.** _____ tens _____ ones
3. _____ tens _____ ones	**4.** _____ ten _____ ones
5. _____ tens _____ ones	**6.** _____ tens _____ ones
7. _____ tens _____ ones	**8.** _____ ten _____ ones
9. _____ ten _____ ones	**10.** _____ tens _____ ones

Place Value: Tens and Ones. Fill in the blanks with the correct number of tens and ones. The first one is done for you.

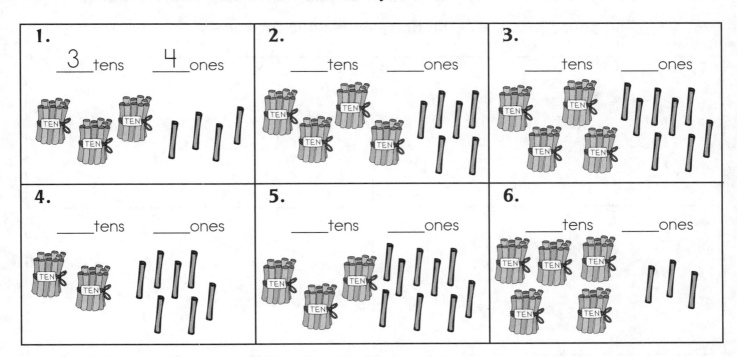

1. __3__ tens __4__ ones

2. _____ tens _____ ones

3. _____ tens _____ ones

4. _____ tens _____ ones

5. _____ tens _____ ones

6. _____ tens _____ ones

Fill in the blanks with the correct number of tens, ones and the total of both together.

Example:

__2__ tens __4__ ones =
__24__

7. _____ ten _____ ones =
_____

8. _____ tens _____ ones =
_____

9. _____ tens _____ ones =
_____

10. _____ tens _____ ones =
_____

11. _____ tens _____ ones =
_____

Name _____

Place Value: Tens and Ones

Draw pictures to show how many tens and how many ones are in each problem.

Use 🔺 o, 📦 | or ▭ □. **The first one is done for you.**

1. 2 tens 4 ones	**2.** 1 tens 6 ones
3. 3 tens 5 ones	**4.** 19

Be sure to read carefully and split each numeral into the correct amount of tens and ones. The first one is done for you.

5. 46 is __4__ tens __6__ ones   **10.** 2 tens, 3 ones is _____

6. 23 is ____ tens ____ ones   **11.** 4 tens, 1 ones is _____

7. 16 is ____ ten ____ ones   **12.** 8 tens, 4 ones is _____

8. 51 is ____ tens ____ one   **13.** 2 ones, 5 tens is _____

9. 83 is ____ ones ____ tens   **14.** 7 tens, 7 ones is _____

 **Circle the one that is greater. The first one is done for you.**

15. 2 tens, 7 ones   **17.** 6 tens, 9 ones   **19.** 9 tens, 9 ones
⟨7 tens, 2 ones⟩   9 tens, 6 ones   9 tens, 8 ones

16. 4 tens, 8 ones   **18.** 5 tens, 3 ones   **20.** 4 tens, 6 ones
8 tens, 4 ones   3 tens, 5 ones   4 tens, 2 ones

Telling Time: Writing Time

Write the time shown on these clocks. The first one is done for you.

1.

_____3_____ o'clock

2.

_____ o'clock

3.

_____ o'clock

4.

_____ o'clock

5.

_____ o'clock

6.

_____ o'clock

Answer the questions below in both clock time and time-of-day descriptions (noon/midnight).

What time is it at noon? _____

What time is it at midnight? _____

What time do most people eat lunch? _____

Telling Time: Drawing Clock Hands

Draw the hands on the clocks to show the time. The first one is done for you.

1.

5:00

2.

8:00

3.

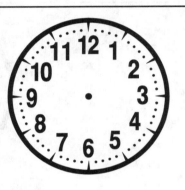

9:00

4.

2:00

5.

10:00

6.

4:00

Keeping Up. Solve each problem. The first one is done for you.

$$\begin{array}{ccccccc}
5 & 7 & 8 & 6 & 9 & 11 & 12 \\
+4 & +2 & +3 & +6 & +3 & +1 & +0 \\
\hline
9 & & & & & &
\end{array}$$

Telling Time: Half-Hour

Write the time shown on these clocks. The first one is done for you.

1.

_7_:30

2.

____:30

3.

____:30

4.

____:30

5.

____:30

6.

_____

7.

_____

8.

_____

What time is it when it is one hour later than 1:00? _____

What time is it one hour earlier than 1:00? _____

Telling Time: Drawing Clock Hands

Draw the hands on the clocks to show the time. The first one is done for you.

1.  1:30	**2.**  3:30	**3.**  8:30
4.  2:30	**5.**  9:30	**6.**  12:30
7.  11:30	**8.**  5:30	**9.**  6:30

Telling Time: Matching

Draw lines to match each clock to the correct time. The first one is done for you.

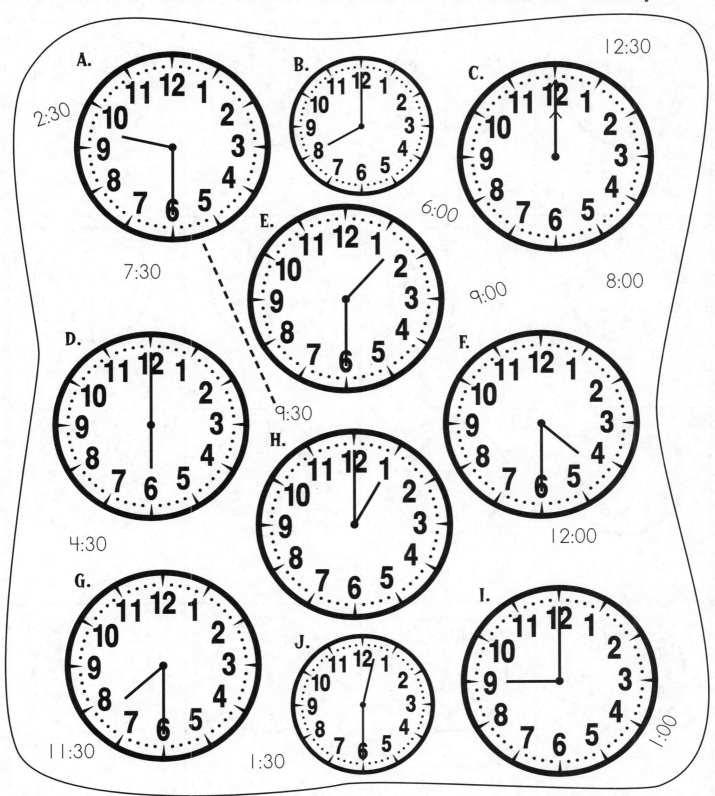

12:30

A.

2:30

B.

C.

7:30

E.

6:00

8:00

9:00

D.

9:30

F.

H.

4:30

12:00

G.

J.

I.

11:30

1:30

1:00

Telling Time: Writing Time

Write the time shown on each clock below. The first one is done for you.

1.  9 : 00	2.  ___ : ___	3.  ___ : ___	4. 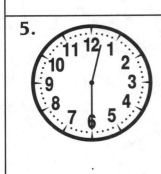 ___ : ___
5. 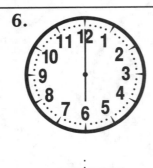 ___ : ___	6.  ___ : ___	7. 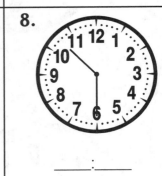 ___ : ___	8. 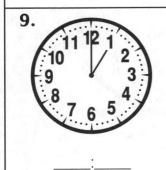 ___ : ___
9. 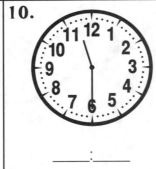 ___ : ___	10.  ___ : ___	11. 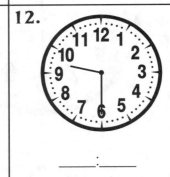 ___ : ___	12. 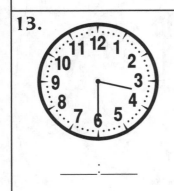 ___ : ___
13. 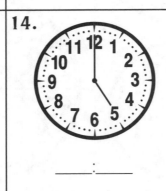 ___ : ___	14.  ___ : ___	15. 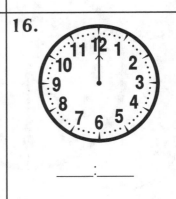 ___ : ___	16. ___ : ___

Number Counting: Counting by 2 and 5

Count by 2's. Color each square yellow that you count by 2.
Start with 0. The first three are done for you.

0	1	2	3	4	5	6	7
8	9	10	11	12	13	14	15
16	17	18	19	20	21	22	23
24	25	26	27	28	29	30	31
32	33	34	35	36	37	38	39
40	41	42	43	44	45	46	47
48	49	50	51	52	53	54	55

Write by 2's to 54. Write the numerals you colored in the above squares.

The first three are done for you.

0   2   4   ___ ___ ___ ___ ___

___ ___ ___ ___ ___ ___ ___ ___

___ ___ ___ ___ ___ ___ ___ ___

___ ___ ___ ___ ___ ___

Counting Circles

Count by 5's. Start with 0 and go to 100. The first three are done for you.

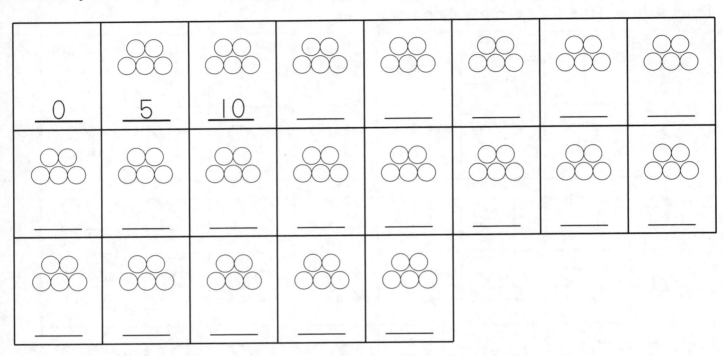

Count by 10's. Start with 0 and go to 100. The first two are done for you.

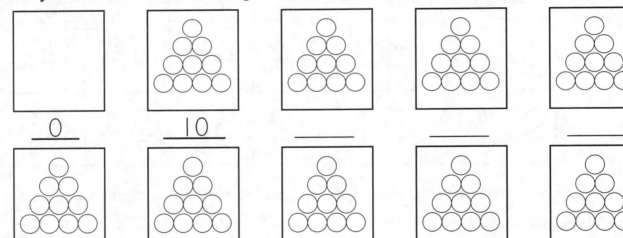

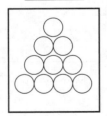

Counting Pennies. Count by 2's. The first two are done for you.

   2   4

_____   _____   _____   _____

_____   _____   _____   _____

_____   _____   _____   _____

Keeping up. An example in each section is done for you.

Circle the number that is greater, or more.

21 (32)	14 10	18 42	16 61
10 11	69 39	24 20	99 89

Circle the number that is less, or fewer.

(1) 11	52 25	90 91	48 84
29 20	71 17	84 85	100 99

Counting Nickels. Count by 5's. The first two are done for you.

5   10   ____   ____

____   ____   ____   ____

____   ____   ____   ____

____   ____   ____   ____

Off the Track

Color all the triangles orange, the circles purple, the rectangles pink and the squares brown.

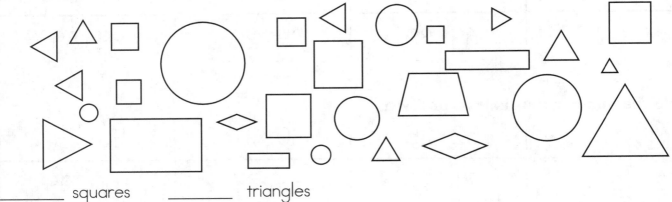

_____ squares   _____ triangles

_____ circles   _____ rectangles   How many shapes are there in all? _____

Counting Dimes. Count by 10's. The first two are done for you.

__10__ __20__ _____ _____ _____ _____

_____ _____ _____ _____

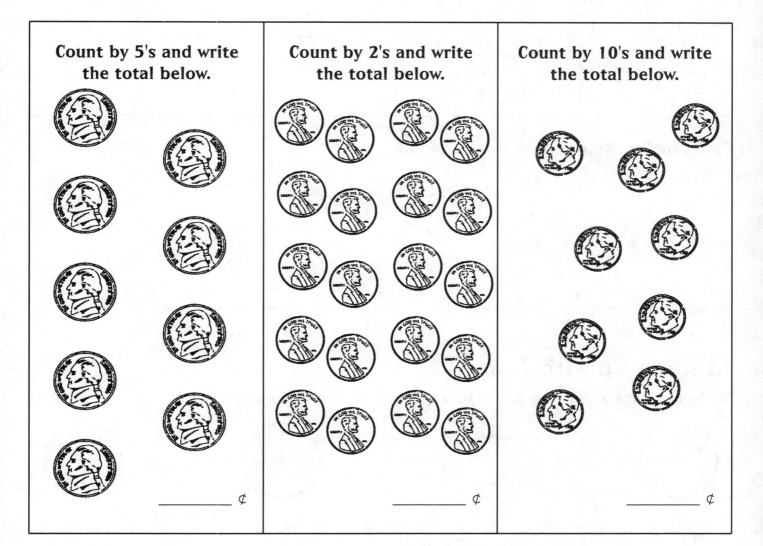

Count by 5's and write the total below.	Count by 2's and write the total below.	Count by 10's and write the total below.
_____ ¢	_____ ¢	_____ ¢

Writing Numerals. **Examples in each section are done for you.**

Count by 2's. Start with 0 and go to 50.

| 0 | 2 | ___ | ___ | ___ | ___ | ___ |

| ___ | ___ | ___ | ___ | ___ | ___ | ___ |

| ___ | ___ | ___ | ___ | ___ | ___ | ___ |

| ___ | ___ | ___ | ___ | ___ | | |

Count by 10's. Start with 0 and go to 100.

| 0 | 10 | ___ | ___ | ___ | ___ | ___ |

| ___ | ___ | ___ | ___ | | | |

Count by 5's. Start with 0 and go to 100.

| 0 | 5 | ___ | ___ | ___ | ___ | ___ |

| ___ | ___ | ___ | ___ | ___ | ___ | ___ |

| ___ | ___ | ___ | ___ | ___ | | |

Keeping Up with Time

Write the time shown on each clock. The first one is done for you.

6:00 _____ _____ _____

Addition 13 —18: Problem Solving

**Count the shapes, add them, and write the total that they make together.
The first one is done for you.**

1.

$$\underline{8} + \underline{5} = \underline{13}$$

2.

$$\underline{} + \underline{} = \underline{}$$

3.

$$\underline{} + \underline{} = \underline{}$$

4.

$$\underline{} + \underline{} = \underline{}$$

5.

$$\underline{} + \underline{} = \underline{}$$

6.

$$\underline{} + \underline{} = \underline{}$$

7.

$$\underline{} + \underline{} = \underline{}$$

8.

$$\underline{} + \underline{} = \underline{}$$

9.

$$\underline{} + \underline{} = \underline{}$$

10.

$$\underline{} + \underline{} = \underline{}$$

Which is longer, a school year or a birthday year?

Underline your answer.

Addition 13 —18: Graphical Problem Solving

Count the shapes, add them, and write the total that they make together.
The first one is done for you.

1.

_15_ + _2_ = _17_

2.

____ + ____ = ____

3.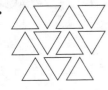

____ + ____ = ____

4.

____ + ____ = ____

5.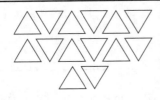

____ + ____ = ____

6.

____ + ____ = ____

7.

____ + ____ = ____

8.

____ + ____ = ____

9.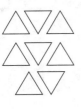

____ + ____ = ____

10.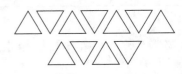

____ + ____ = ____

Addition 13 —18: Number Match

Solve the problems below. Next find the problems that equal the same amount and draw a line to match them. The first one is done for you.

1. $6 + 7 \ = \ \underline{13}$ $1 + 13 = \underline{}$

$3 + 12 = \underline{}$ $9 + 7 \ = \ \underline{}$

$8 + 6 \ = \ \underline{}$ $1 + 12 = \underline{13}$

$0 + 16 = \underline{}$ $2 + 15 = \underline{}$

$8 + 10 = \underline{}$ $9 + 6 \ = \ \underline{}$

$9 + 8 \ = \ \underline{}$ $1 + 17 = \underline{}$

2. $2 + 12 = \underline{}$ $14 + 1 \ = \ \underline{}$

$2 + 13 = \underline{}$ $4 + 12 = \underline{}$

$2 + 11 = \underline{}$ $14 + 0 \ = \ \underline{}$

$13 + 4 \ = \ \underline{}$ $1 + 17 = \underline{}$

$10 + 6 \ = \ \underline{}$ $13 + 4 \ = \ \underline{}$

$7 + 11 = \underline{}$ $12 + 1 \ = \ \underline{}$

3. $10 + 8 \ = \ \underline{}$ $18 + 0 \ = \ \underline{}$

$3 + 11 = \underline{}$ $1 + 16 = \underline{}$

$2 + 14 = \underline{}$ $13 + 2 \ = \ \underline{}$

$6 + 11 = \underline{}$ $10 + 3 \ = \ \underline{}$

$5 + 10 = \underline{}$ $7 + 9 \ = \ \underline{}$

$5 + 8 \ = \ \underline{}$ $9 + 5 \ = \ \underline{}$

4. $1 + 15 = \underline{}$ $15 + 3 \ = \ \underline{}$

$0 + 13 = \underline{}$ $11 + 4 \ = \ \underline{}$

$5 + 13 = \underline{}$ $6 + 10 = \underline{}$

$5 + 9 \ = \ \underline{}$ $13 + 1 \ = \ \underline{}$

$4 + 11 = \underline{}$ $17 + 0 \ = \ \underline{}$

$14 + 3 \ = \ \underline{}$ $11 + 2 \ = \ \underline{}$

5. $10 + 7 \ = \ \underline{}$ $2 + 15 = \underline{}$

$7 + 7 \ = \ \underline{}$ $0 + 14 = \underline{}$

$3 + 13 = \underline{}$ $14 + 2 \ = \ \underline{}$

$13 + 5 \ = \ \underline{}$ $2 + 16 = \underline{}$

$4 + 9 \ = \ \underline{}$ $10 + 3 \ = \ \underline{}$

$0 + 15 = \underline{}$ $7 + 8 \ = \ \underline{}$

6. $10 + 5 \ = \ \underline{}$ $16 + 2 \ = \ \underline{}$

$7 + 6 \ = \ \underline{}$ $15 + 1 \ = \ \underline{}$

$0 + 18 = \underline{}$ $12 + 3 \ = \ \underline{}$

$4 + 13 = \underline{}$ $12 + 2 \ = \ \underline{}$

$12 + 4 \ = \ \underline{}$ $4 + 9 \ = \ \underline{}$

$4 + 10 = \underline{}$ $5 + 12 = \underline{}$

7. $15 + 0 \ = \ \underline{}$ $5 + 11 = \underline{}$

$14 + 4 \ = \ \underline{}$ $16 + 1 \ = \ \underline{}$

$13 + 3 \ = \ \underline{}$ $6 + 9 \ = \ \underline{}$

$0 + 17 = \underline{}$ $9 + 5 \ = \ \underline{}$

$5 + 8 \ = \ \underline{}$ $6 + 7 \ = \ \underline{}$

$7 + 7 \ = \ \underline{}$ $9 + 9 \ = \ \underline{}$

8. $9 + 6 \ = \ \underline{}$ $0 + 16 = \underline{}$

$11 + 6 \ = \ \underline{}$ $14 + 2 \ = \ \underline{}$

$2 + 16 = \underline{}$ $17 + 0 \ = \ \underline{}$

$8 + 8 \ = \ \underline{}$ $8 + 7 \ = \ \underline{}$

$5 + 9 \ = \ \underline{}$ $11 + 7 \ = \ \underline{}$

$16 + 0 \ = \ \underline{}$ $2 + 12 = \underline{}$

Addition 13 — 18: More Problem Solving
Find the sums. The first one is done for you.

1.

5	6	15	15	3	1
+9	+9	+3	+2	+11	+12
14					

2.

3	10	4	7	8	0
+13	+8	+13	+6	+8	+16

3.

11	6	2	13	7	8
+3	+12	+15	+5	+7	+5

4.

6	1	3	7	7	6
+10	+14	+10	+11	+9	+8

5.

5	5	9	7	16	9
+8	+10	+9	+10	+2	+7

6.

9	10	12	9	9	6
+4	+6	+6	+6	+8	+7

7.

12	11	8	11	7	0
+4	+2	+10	+7	+8	+14

Addition 13 —18: Word Problem Solving

Read the story and solve the problem. The first one is done for you.

1. John ate 3 peanuts. Then he ate 10 more. How many peanuts did he eat in all?

___3___ + ___10___ = ___13___

2. Julie has 4 story books. Her brother has 11. How many books do they have all together?

_____ + _____ = _____

3. Rick has 5 cats and his friend has 12 dogs. How many pets do they have in all?

_____ + _____ = _____

4. Nan used 2 cans of paint on the dog house. She used 13 on the fence. How many cans of paint did she use all together?

_____ + _____ = _____

5. David walked 8 miles on Monday and 7 miles on Tuesday. How far did he walk all together?

_____ + _____ = _____

6. Our class had a picnic. We had 8 girls and 9 boys at the picnic. How many boys and girls were there in all?

_____ + _____ = _____

7. 9 lions live in the zoo. 5 tigers are there too. How many total lions and tigers live in the zoo?

```
  9
+ 5
___
```

8. A monkey ate 11 bananas for lunch. He ate 5 for a snack. How many did he eat in all?

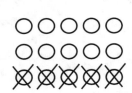

Subtraction 13 — 18: Problem Solving

Count the shapes that are crossed off, then subtract this amount from the total number of shapes to solve each problem. The first one is done for you.

1. 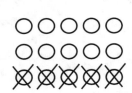 $15 - \underline{5} = \underline{10}$	**2.** 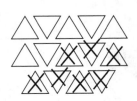 $14 - \underline{} = \underline{}$	**3.** 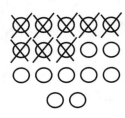 $17 - \underline{} = \underline{}$
4. 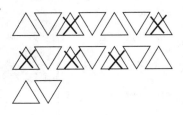 $16 - \underline{} = \underline{}$	**5.** 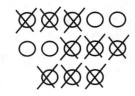 $13 - \underline{} = \underline{}$	**6.** 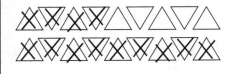 $18 - \underline{} = \underline{}$
7. 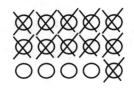 $15 - \underline{} = \underline{}$	**8.**  $14 - \underline{} = \underline{}$	**9.** 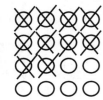 $16 - \underline{} = \underline{}$
10. 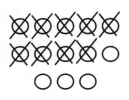 $13 - \underline{} = \underline{}$	**11.** 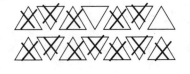 $14 - \underline{} = \underline{}$	**12.** 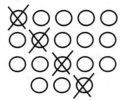 $18 - \underline{} = \underline{}$

Name _____

Subtraction 13 — 18: Comparison. Circle all the other problems
that equal the same numeral in the box. The first two are done for you.

1.

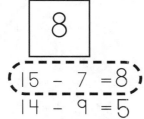

15 – 7 = 8
14 – 9 = 5
14 – 6 =
18 – 10 =
17 – 4 =
17 – 9 =

2.

18 – 14 =
13 – 9 =
15 – 8 =
16 – 12 =
15 – 10 =
14 – 0 =

3.

18 – 18 =
18 – 8 =
15 – 0 =
16 – 6 =
14 – 4 =
13 – 3 =

4.

13

16 – 3 =
13 – 0 =
18 – 5 =
15 – 2 =
16 – 2 =
13 – 2 =

5.

16 – 13 =
16 – 16 =
15 – 0 =
13 – 13 =
18 – 7 =
17 – 17 =

6.

2

18 – 16 =
16 – 9 =
15 – 13 =
14 – 8 =
13 – 11 =
17 – 16 =

7.

1

17 – 16 =
15 – 13 =
14 – 13 =
16 – 15 =
18 – 17 =
17 – 12 =

8.

5

14 – 9 =
15 – 0 =
13 – 1 =
16 – 11 =
17 – 12 =
13 – 8 =

9.

11

17 – 15 =
18 – 18 =
17 – 6 =
15 – 4 =
13 – 2 =
14 – 0 =

Subtraction 13 — 18: Problem Solving

Write the difference for each problem below. The first one is done for you.

1.
$$\begin{array}{r} 16 \\ -4 \\ \hline 12 \end{array} \quad \begin{array}{r} 14 \\ -10 \\ \hline \end{array} \quad \begin{array}{r} 13 \\ -3 \\ \hline \end{array} \quad \begin{array}{r} 18 \\ -7 \\ \hline \end{array} \quad \begin{array}{r} 15 \\ -8 \\ \hline \end{array} \quad \begin{array}{r} 14 \\ -5 \\ \hline \end{array}$$

2.
$$\begin{array}{r} 14 \\ -14 \\ \hline \end{array} \quad \begin{array}{r} 18 \\ -6 \\ \hline \end{array} \quad \begin{array}{r} 17 \\ -5 \\ \hline \end{array} \quad \begin{array}{r} 17 \\ -11 \\ \hline \end{array} \quad \begin{array}{r} 14 \\ -8 \\ \hline \end{array} \quad \begin{array}{r} 16 \\ -9 \\ \hline \end{array}$$

3.
$$\begin{array}{r} 13 \\ -7 \\ \hline \end{array} \quad \begin{array}{r} 16 \\ -7 \\ \hline \end{array} \quad \begin{array}{r} 13 \\ -0 \\ \hline \end{array} \quad \begin{array}{r} 18 \\ -15 \\ \hline \end{array} \quad \begin{array}{r} 18 \\ -18 \\ \hline \end{array} \quad \begin{array}{r} 14 \\ -7 \\ \hline \end{array}$$

4.
$$\begin{array}{r} 15 \\ -9 \\ \hline \end{array} \quad \begin{array}{r} 18 \\ -1 \\ \hline \end{array} \quad \begin{array}{r} 13 \\ -5 \\ \hline \end{array} \quad \begin{array}{r} 16 \\ -8 \\ \hline \end{array} \quad \begin{array}{r} 15 \\ -3 \\ \hline \end{array} \quad \begin{array}{r} 14 \\ -11 \\ \hline \end{array}$$

5.
$$\begin{array}{r} 13 \\ -6 \\ \hline \end{array} \quad \begin{array}{r} 18 \\ -9 \\ \hline \end{array} \quad \begin{array}{r} 18 \\ -0 \\ \hline \end{array} \quad \begin{array}{r} 17 \\ -7 \\ \hline \end{array} \quad \begin{array}{r} 14 \\ -3 \\ \hline \end{array} \quad \begin{array}{r} 15 \\ -0 \\ \hline \end{array}$$

6.
$$\begin{array}{r} 15 \\ -6 \\ \hline \end{array} \quad \begin{array}{r} 13 \\ -1 \\ \hline \end{array} \quad \begin{array}{r} 17 \\ -15 \\ \hline \end{array} \quad \begin{array}{r} 18 \\ -2 \\ \hline \end{array} \quad \begin{array}{r} 15 \\ -1 \\ \hline \end{array} \quad \begin{array}{r} 13 \\ -10 \\ \hline \end{array}$$

7.
$$\begin{array}{r} 18 \\ -11 \\ \hline \end{array} \quad \begin{array}{r} 17 \\ -3 \\ \hline \end{array} \quad \begin{array}{r} 16 \\ -0 \\ \hline \end{array} \quad \begin{array}{r} 15 \\ -9 \\ \hline \end{array} \quad \begin{array}{r} 16 \\ -13 \\ \hline \end{array} \quad \begin{array}{r} 13 \\ -12 \\ \hline \end{array}$$

Name _____

Subtraction Picture

Write the differences and color the picture using the coloring key below the picture.

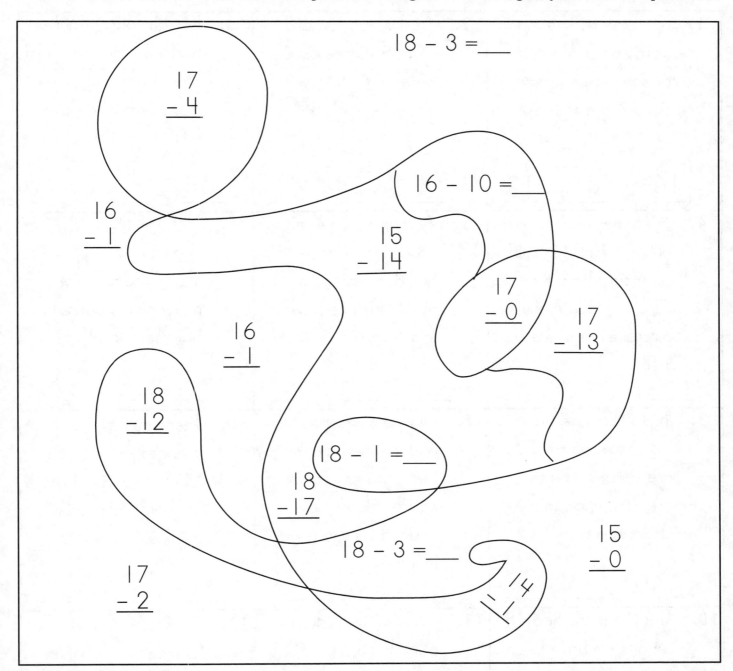

Coloring Key. The answer for each difference above determines how you color each area of the picture.

Answer: 17 – color: blue • Answer: 6 – color: black • Answer: 4 – color: orange
Answer: 13 – color: red • Answer: 1 – color: green • Answer: 15 – color: yellow

Word Problem Solving. Read the story and solve the problem.

The first one is done for you.

1. Sue had 16 spelling words on her test. She missed 3. How many did she get right? $\underline{16} - \underline{3} = \underline{13}$	**2.** At the zoo Richard saw 14 monkeys. 6 were brown. How many were black? $\underline{14} - \underline{6} = \underline{\hphantom{00}}$	**3.** For her party Lauren had 13 balloons. 5 of them blew away. How many does she have left? $\underline{13} - \underline{\hphantom{00}} = \underline{\hphantom{00}}$
4. A farmer had 15 pigs on his farm. He sold 7 of them to another farmer. How many pigs does he have left? $\underline{\hphantom{00}} - \underline{\hphantom{00}} = \underline{\hphantom{00}}$	**5.** Andy had 16 math problems to do. He has done 9. How many does he have left to do? $\underline{\hphantom{00}} - \underline{\hphantom{00}} = \underline{\hphantom{00}}$	**6.** Mrs. Hill had 18 plants in a box. She planted 12 of them. How many plants does she have left to plant? $\underline{\hphantom{00}} - \underline{\hphantom{00}} = \underline{\hphantom{00}}$
7. In our class we have 13 chairs. 6 of them are yellow. The rest are red. How many chairs are red? $\underline{\hphantom{00}} - \underline{\hphantom{00}} = \underline{\hphantom{00}}$	**8.** Marge works for 17 hours. She has already been at work for 4 hours. How many hours does she have left to work? $\underline{\hphantom{00}} - \underline{\hphantom{00}} = \underline{\hphantom{00}}$	**9.** There were 14 oranges in the basket. My friends and I ate 5 of them. How many oranges are left? $\underline{\hphantom{00}} - \underline{\hphantom{00}} = \underline{\hphantom{00}}$
10. The pet store had 18 rabbits. 9 have been sold. How many are left to sell? $\underline{\hphantom{00}} - \underline{\hphantom{00}} = \underline{\hphantom{00}}$	**11.** 15 boys were playing ball. 4 boys went inside. How many boys are still outside playing ball? $\underline{\hphantom{00}} - \underline{\hphantom{00}} = \underline{\hphantom{00}}$	**12.** 17 wild horses were running. 13 of them stopped to drink. How many did not stop? $\underline{\hphantom{00}} - \underline{\hphantom{00}} = \underline{\hphantom{00}}$

Subtraction 13 — 18: More Problem Solving

Write each difference. The first one is done for you.

1.
$$\begin{array}{r} 17 \\ -11 \\ \hline 6 \end{array} \qquad \begin{array}{r} 18 \\ -4 \\ \hline \end{array} \qquad \begin{array}{r} 13 \\ -5 \\ \hline \end{array} \qquad \begin{array}{r} 16 \\ -7 \\ \hline \end{array} \qquad \begin{array}{r} 15 \\ -14 \\ \hline \end{array} \qquad \begin{array}{r} 14 \\ -4 \\ \hline \end{array}$$

2.
$$\begin{array}{r} 14 \\ -6 \\ \hline \end{array} \qquad \begin{array}{r} 16 \\ -10 \\ \hline \end{array} \qquad \begin{array}{r} 18 \\ -9 \\ \hline \end{array} \qquad \begin{array}{r} 17 \\ -4 \\ \hline \end{array} \qquad \begin{array}{r} 13 \\ -10 \\ \hline \end{array} \qquad \begin{array}{r} 15 \\ -6 \\ \hline \end{array}$$

3.
$$\begin{array}{r} 15 \\ -10 \\ \hline \end{array} \qquad \begin{array}{r} 16 \\ -11 \\ \hline \end{array} \qquad \begin{array}{r} 18 \\ -8 \\ \hline \end{array} \qquad \begin{array}{r} 14 \\ -13 \\ \hline \end{array} \qquad \begin{array}{r} 16 \\ -16 \\ \hline \end{array} \qquad \begin{array}{r} 17 \\ -8 \\ \hline \end{array}$$

4.
$$\begin{array}{r} 16 \\ -8 \\ \hline \end{array} \qquad \begin{array}{r} 14 \\ -8 \\ \hline \end{array} \qquad \begin{array}{r} 13 \\ -8 \\ \hline \end{array} \qquad \begin{array}{r} 17 \\ -10 \\ \hline \end{array} \qquad \begin{array}{r} 15 \\ -7 \\ \hline \end{array} \qquad \begin{array}{r} 18 \\ -18 \\ \hline \end{array}$$

5.
$$\begin{array}{r} 18 \\ -6 \\ \hline \end{array} \qquad \begin{array}{r} 15 \\ -9 \\ \hline \end{array} \qquad \begin{array}{r} 13 \\ -2 \\ \hline \end{array} \qquad \begin{array}{r} 16 \\ -6 \\ \hline \end{array} \qquad \begin{array}{r} 17 \\ -12 \\ \hline \end{array} \qquad \begin{array}{r} 14 \\ -5 \\ \hline \end{array}$$

6.
$$\begin{array}{r} 13 \\ -0 \\ \hline \end{array} \qquad \begin{array}{r} 17 \\ -7 \\ \hline \end{array} \qquad \begin{array}{r} 17 \\ -3 \\ \hline \end{array} \qquad \begin{array}{r} 18 \\ -16 \\ \hline \end{array} \qquad \begin{array}{r} 18 \\ -7 \\ \hline \end{array} \qquad \begin{array}{r} 13 \\ -9 \\ \hline \end{array}$$

Keeping Up. **Count to 70 by 5's. The first one is done for you.**

  5   ____   ____   ____   ____   ____

____   ____   ____   ____   ____   ____

Name _____

Subtraction 13 — 18: More Problem Solving

Write each difference. The first one is done for you.

1.	2.	3.
14 – 9 = __5__	16 – 4 = _____	15 – 12 = _____
16 – 9 = _____	18 – 17 = _____	14 – 7 = _____
18 – 3 = _____	17 – 9 = _____	18 – 8 = _____
15 – 8 = _____	18 – 12 = _____	14 – 0 = _____
16 – 3 = _____	17 – 15 = _____	15 – 13 = _____
14 – 0 = _____	15 – 4 = _____	14 – 11 = _____

4.	5.	6.
13 – 1 = _____	15 – 0 = _____	18 – 1 = _____
15 – 5 = _____	18 – 11 = _____	14 – 2 = _____
16 – 4 = _____	17 – 13 = _____	16 – 1 = _____
18 – 5 = _____	14 – 10 = _____	18 – 13 = _____
14 – 11 = _____	13 – 11 = _____	16 – 14 = _____
16 – 15 = _____	16 – 13 = _____	17 – 10 = _____

7.	8.	9.
13 – 3 = _____	13 – 12 = _____	14 – 1 = _____
15 – 1 = _____	16 – 0 = _____	13 – 13 = _____
16 – 12 = _____	18 – 2 = _____	16 – 2 = _____
17 – 14 = _____	17 – 5 = _____	18 – 2 = _____
18 – 0 = _____	18 – 4 = _____	17 – 16 = _____
13 – 4 = _____	13 – 7 = _____	18 – 15 = _____

10.	11.	12.
14 – 3 = _____	17 – 17 = _____	14 – 12 = _____
15 – 2 = _____	15 – 3 = _____	15 – 4 = _____
17 – 1 = _____	14 – 14 = _____	17 – 2 = _____
14 – 12 = _____	17 – 6 = _____	16 – 7 = _____
15 – 15 = _____	15 – 14 = _____	17 – 0 = _____

Money: Counting Coins. Count the coins and write the total amount of money their combination makes. The first one is done for you.

1.

8 ____ ¢

2.

_____ ¢

3.

_____ ¢

4.

_____ ¢

5.

_____ ¢

6.

_____ ¢

7.

_____ ¢

8.

_____ ¢

9.

_____ ¢

10.

_____ ¢

Money: Counting Coins.
Circle a correct combination of coins that equals the amount of money shown in the box. The first one is done for you.

1. 15¢

2. 25¢

3. 32¢

4. 16¢

5. 45¢

6. 29¢

7. 60¢

8. 11¢

Money: Dividing Money
Fill in the blanks to make each comparison true. The first one is done for you.

1. 3 dimes equals __30__ ¢

2. 1 nickel equals _____ ¢

3. 1 dime, 1 nickel equals _____ ¢

4. 1 penny is _____ ¢

5. 2 nickels equals _____ ¢

6. 40¢ is how many dimes? _____

7. 6¢ is _____ nickel and _____ penny.

8. 5 nickels equals _____ ¢

9. 15¢ is _____ nickels or _____ dime _____ nickel.

10. 1 quarter is _____ ¢

11. 5 dimes is _____ ¢

12. 6 nickels is _____ ¢

13. 21¢ can be _____ dimes and _____ penny or _____ pennies.

14. 25¢ can be _____ quarter or _____ dimes and _____ nickel.

15. 10¢ can be _____ pennies or _____ dime or _____ nickels.

Tell how much money is in each row. The first one is done for you.

1.

_____39_____ ¢

2.

_____ ¢

3.

_____ ¢

4.
_____ ¢

Money Practice.
On the line next to each toy write the letter that stands for the amount of money that each toy costs. The first one is done for you.

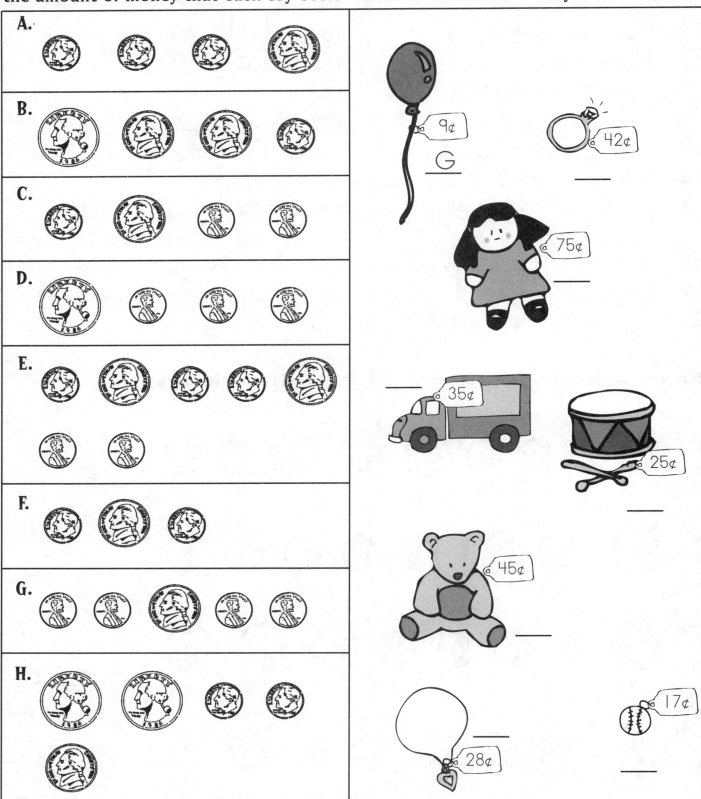

A.

B.

C.

D.

E.

F.

G.

H.

9¢

G

42¢

75¢ ___

35¢ ___

25¢

___

45¢ ___

28¢ ___

17¢

___

Word Problem Solving.

Solve the problems by placing an addition or sub-traction sign in the circle and by filling in the blanks. The first one is done for you.

1. I found 10¢ on the sidewalk. My mom gave me a nickel. How much money do I have now? 10¢ ⊕ 5¢ = 15¢	**2.** Harlee spent 9¢ for an apple and 4¢ for a stamp. How much did she spend in all? 9¢ ◯ 4¢ = 13¢	**3.** Tom had 18¢. He spent 9¢. How much does he have left? 18¢ ◯ 9¢ = 9¢
4. A banana costs 10¢ and an orange is 8¢. How much do they cost together? 10¢ ◯ ___ = ___	**5.** Mary had 15¢. She lost 4¢. How much does she have left? 15¢ ◯ ___ = ___	**6.** At the book sale Sarah bought two books. One was 14¢ the other cost 3¢. How much did she spend in all? 14¢ ◯ ___ = ___
7. Sam had 2 dimes and 1 nickel. How much money does he have in all? 20¢ ◯ ___ = ___	**8.** Brittany had 16 pennies. She gave 8 of them to Joe. How many pennies does she have left? ___ ◯ 8¢ = ___	**9.** One toy car costs 8¢. How much will two cars cost? ___ ◯ 8¢ = ___
10. I have 15¢. I want to buy an ice cream cone for 10¢. How much will I have left? ___ ◯ 10¢ = ___	**11.** Trace made 6¢ on Monday and 8¢ on Tuesday. How much did he make in all? ___ ◯ 8¢ = ___	**12.** Emily had 17¢. She put 9¢ in her bank. How much does she have left? ___ ◯ 9¢ = ___

 Write the number sentence for the coins below.

       ___ – ___ = ___

Name _____

Adding Doubles

Solve the problems below. The first one is done for you.

1.
$\begin{array}{r} 1 \\ +1 \\ \hline 2 \end{array}$
$\begin{array}{r} 9 \\ +9 \\ \hline \end{array}$
$\begin{array}{r} 7 \\ +7 \\ \hline \end{array}$
$\begin{array}{r} 2 \\ +2 \\ \hline \end{array}$
$\begin{array}{r} 4 \\ +4 \\ \hline \end{array}$
$\begin{array}{r} 9 \\ +9 \\ \hline \end{array}$

2.
$\begin{array}{r} 3 \\ +3 \\ \hline \end{array}$
$\begin{array}{r} 0 \\ +0 \\ \hline \end{array}$
$\begin{array}{r} 5 \\ +5 \\ \hline \end{array}$
$\begin{array}{r} 8 \\ +8 \\ \hline \end{array}$
$\begin{array}{r} 10 \\ +10 \\ \hline \end{array}$
$\begin{array}{r} 6 \\ +6 \\ \hline \end{array}$

3.
$\begin{array}{r} 7 \\ +7 \\ \hline \end{array}$
$\begin{array}{r} 1 \\ +1 \\ \hline \end{array}$
$\begin{array}{r} 11 \\ +11 \\ \hline \end{array}$
$\begin{array}{r} 5 \\ +5 \\ \hline \end{array}$
$\begin{array}{r} 2 \\ +2 \\ \hline \end{array}$
$\begin{array}{r} 4 \\ +4 \\ \hline \end{array}$

4.
$\begin{array}{r} 3 \\ +3 \\ \hline \end{array}$
$\begin{array}{r} 12 \\ +12 \\ \hline \end{array}$
$\begin{array}{r} 6 \\ +6 \\ \hline \end{array}$
$\begin{array}{r} 8 \\ +8 \\ \hline \end{array}$
$\begin{array}{r} 0 \\ +0 \\ \hline \end{array}$
$\begin{array}{r} 10 \\ +10 \\ \hline \end{array}$

Complete these number families. The first one is done for you.

1.
12 2
14

$2 + 12 = 14$
$12 + 2 = 14$
$14 - 12 = 2$
$14 - 2 = 12$

2.
11 16
5

___ + ___ = ___
___ + ___ = ___
___ - ___ = ___
___ - ___ = ___

3.
10 8
18

___ + ___ = ___
___ + ___ = ___
___ - ___ = ___
___ - ___ = ___

4.
13 5
8

___ + ___ = ___
___ + ___ = ___
___ - ___ = ___
___ - ___ = ___

Addition 0 — 18: Problem Solving

Write each sum. The first one is done for you.

1.	5 + 7 12	10 + 6	4 + 0	1 + 3	2 + 8	5 + 11

2.	3 + 1	5 + 2	6 + 9	12 + 1	11 + 5	7 + 4

3.	0 + 5	2 + 8	1 + 11	2 + 15	16 + 1	5 + 5

4.	10 + 1	3 + 7	9 + 2	3 + 2	1 + 4	4 + 7

5.	14 + 3	5 + 3	2 + 6	12 + 6	6 + 4	2 + 3

What order are these fish in? Write your answer below each fish. The first one is done for you.

first	_____	_____	_____	_____
fifth	fourth	first	second	third

Subtraction 0 — 18: Problem Solving

Write each difference. The first one is done for you.

1.
```
 12      8     11      6      3     11
-10     -7    -10     -4     -2     -3
_____
  2
```

2.
```
  7     14      4     10      8     15
 -5     -7     -3     -9     -8     -6
```

3.
```
  9     12      2      6     13     16
 -8     -2     -0     -1     -6     -7
```

4.
```
  5     10      8      7      5     18
 -2    -10     -5     -3     -5     -7
```

5.
```
  6     12      9     17      9      4
 -3     -4     -6     -8     -9     -2
```

Circle the fraction that describes the shaded part of each shape. The first one is done for you.

1.

$$\frac{1}{2} \quad \frac{1}{3} \quad \frac{1}{4}$$

2.

$$\frac{1}{3} \quad \frac{1}{2} \quad \frac{2}{3}$$

3.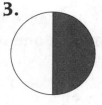

$$\frac{1}{2} \quad \frac{1}{3} \quad \frac{1}{4}$$

4.

$$\frac{1}{2} \quad \frac{3}{4} \quad \frac{2}{4}$$

5.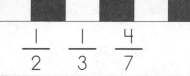

$$\frac{1}{2} \quad \frac{1}{3} \quad \frac{4}{7}$$

Addition 0 — 18: More Problem Solving

Write each sum. The first one is done for you.

1. 0 + 0 = __0__	**2.** 8 + 1 = ____	**3.** 1 + 5 = ____
4 + 9 = ____	9 + 3 = ____	0 + 3 = ____
3 + 11 = ____	6 + 8 = ____	3 + 8 = ____
1 + 9 = ____	4 + 1 = ____	2 + 7 = ____
0 + 7 = ____	6 + 0 = ____	5 + 4 = ____
7 + 3 = ____	8 + 2 = ____	12 + 0 = ____
4. 1 + 7 = ____	**5.** 4 + 2 = ____	**6.** 3 + 6 = ____
5 + 5 = ____	5 + 1 = ____	10 + 4 = ____
8 + 0 = ____	8 + 3 = ____	8 + 7 = ____
3 + 3 = ____	2 + 6 = ____	14 + 0 = ____
9 + 4 = ____	9 + 5 = ____	1 + 1 = ____
3 + 13 = ____	0 + 8 = ____	2 + 2 = ____
7. 6 + 2 = ____	**8.** 0 + 2 = ____	**9.** 0 + 4 = ____
5 + 7 = ____	2 + 6 = ____	1 + 2 = ____
0 + 1 = ____	4 + 5 = ____	5 + 7 = ____
2 + 1 = ____	7 + 1 = ____	6 + 1 = ____
3 + 4 = ____	6 + 11 = ____	8 + 4 = ____
11 + 1 = ____	2 + 16 = ____	13 + 5 = ____

 **Measure each line using a centimeter ruler. Write the length in the blank. The first one is done for you.**

1. _____ __9__ cm   4. _____ _____ cm

2. _____ _____ cm   5. _____

_____ cm

3. _____ 6. _____

_____ cm   _____ cm

Subtraction 0 — 18: More Problem Solving

Write each difference. The first one is done for you.

1. 6 – 5 = 1	**2.** 8 – 3 = ___	**3.** 3 – 3 = ___
4 – 4 = ___	7 – 2 = ___	18 – 10 = ___
10 – 6 = ___	12 – 1 = ___	14 – 6 = ___
9 – 3 = ___	9 – 7 = ___	9 – 5 = ___
7 – 7 = ___	6 – 2 = ___	8 – 4 = ___
2 – 1 = ___	4 – 0 = ___	6 – 6 = ___
4. 12 – 9 = ___	**5.** 6 – 0 = ___	**6.** 0 – 0 = ___
7 – 6 = ___	13 – 11 = ___	12 – 8 = ___
14 – 10 = ___	16 – 4 = ___	15 – 2 = ___
13 – 9 = ___	1 – 1 = ___	9 – 1 = ___
10 – 3 = ___	10 – 1 = ___	7 – 4 = ___
8 – 2 = ___	8 – 0 = ___	12 – 11 = ___
7. 5 – 3 = ___	**8.** 15 – 9 = ___	**9.** 5 – 1 = ___
1 – 0 = ___	17 – 14 = ___	18 – 4 = ___
12 – 7 = ___	11 – 8 = ___	9 – 4 = ___
7 – 1 = ___	5 – 4 = ___	11 – 2 = ___
10 – 8 = ___	18 – 2 = ___	8 – 7 = ___
14 – 11 = ___	5 – 0 = ___	4 – 1 = ___

Measure each line using a inch ruler. Write the length in the blank. The first one is done for you.

1. ————————————

          __2__ in

4. —————————————————

        ____ in

2. ——————————————————

3. ————————

      ____ in

5. ———————————————————

        ____ in

6. ——————————————————————

       ____ in

Addition 0 — 18: Column Addition

Solve the problems below.   The first one is done for you.

1.

2	6	5	4	9	2
1	1	8	0	2	2
+ 3	+ 0	+ 2	+ 2	+ 2	+ 2
6					

2.

1	10	6	4	2	7
0	3	6	4	7	3
+ 5	+ 1	+ 6	+ 4	+ 2	+ 3

3.

3	0	5	1	2	3
3	12	8	9	3	2
+ 3	+ 2	+ 2	+ 3	+ 4	+ 3

4.

4	3	2	1	4	6
8	9	8	3	4	1
+ 2	+ 4	+ 5	+ 1	+ 0	+ 1

5.

2	9	6	5	3	7
2	0	3	5	9	0
+ 3	+ 0	+ 3	+ 5	+ 6	+ 7

6.

0	1	11	10	4	8
8	5	2	6	3	3
+ 4	+ 4	+ 2	+ 1	+ 10	+ 0

Addition 0 — 18: 2-Digit Numeral Addition

Solve the problems below. The first one is done for you.

1.	12	61	24	10	25	32
	+ 13	+ 17	+ 11	+ 19	+ 14	+ 12
	25					

2.	11	42	33	51	42	13
	+ 10	+ 16	+ 22	+ 16	+ 21	+ 13

3.	14	52	21	14	39	40
	+ 12	+ 15	+ 35	+ 81	+ 30	+ 51

4.	36	14	37	10	13	20
	+ 12	+ 15	+ 21	+ 74	+ 86	+ 10

5.	10	23	15	30	18	10
	+ 89	+ 55	+ 14	+ 60	+ 41	+ 10

Brain Work Measure each part of the line using an inch ruler, write the length of each part, and then add these lengths to find the total length.

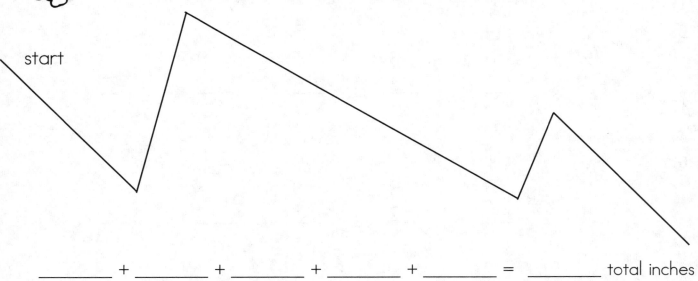

start

_____ + _____ + _____ + _____ + _____ = _____ total inches

Subtraction 0 — 18: 2-Digit Numeral Subtraction

Solve the problems below. The first one is done for you.

1.
$$\begin{array}{r} 24 \\ -11 \\ \hline 13 \end{array}$$
$$\begin{array}{r} 36 \\ -14 \\ \hline \end{array}$$
$$\begin{array}{r} 32 \\ -12 \\ \hline \end{array}$$
$$\begin{array}{r} 68 \\ -21 \\ \hline \end{array}$$
$$\begin{array}{r} 92 \\ -31 \\ \hline \end{array}$$
$$\begin{array}{r} 77 \\ -66 \\ \hline \end{array}$$

2.
$$\begin{array}{r} 18 \\ -10 \\ \hline \end{array}$$
$$\begin{array}{r} 88 \\ -44 \\ \hline \end{array}$$
$$\begin{array}{r} 69 \\ -33 \\ \hline \end{array}$$
$$\begin{array}{r} 25 \\ -13 \\ \hline \end{array}$$
$$\begin{array}{r} 78 \\ -47 \\ \hline \end{array}$$
$$\begin{array}{r} 94 \\ -82 \\ \hline \end{array}$$

3.
$$\begin{array}{r} 90 \\ -20 \\ \hline \end{array}$$
$$\begin{array}{r} 12 \\ -12 \\ \hline \end{array}$$
$$\begin{array}{r} 83 \\ -72 \\ \hline \end{array}$$
$$\begin{array}{r} 66 \\ -34 \\ \hline \end{array}$$
$$\begin{array}{r} 29 \\ -19 \\ \hline \end{array}$$
$$\begin{array}{r} 78 \\ -34 \\ \hline \end{array}$$

4.
$$\begin{array}{r} 51 \\ -10 \\ \hline \end{array}$$
$$\begin{array}{r} 82 \\ -71 \\ \hline \end{array}$$
$$\begin{array}{r} 49 \\ -32 \\ \hline \end{array}$$
$$\begin{array}{r} 55 \\ -22 \\ \hline \end{array}$$
$$\begin{array}{r} 95 \\ -23 \\ \hline \end{array}$$
$$\begin{array}{r} 62 \\ -41 \\ \hline \end{array}$$

5.
$$\begin{array}{r} 89 \\ -10 \\ \hline \end{array}$$
$$\begin{array}{r} 60 \\ -30 \\ \hline \end{array}$$
$$\begin{array}{r} 57 \\ -34 \\ \hline \end{array}$$
$$\begin{array}{r} 26 \\ -16 \\ \hline \end{array}$$
$$\begin{array}{r} 44 \\ -13 \\ \hline \end{array}$$
$$\begin{array}{r} 99 \\ -86 \\ \hline \end{array}$$

Place Value in Tens and Ones. **Read carefully and fill in the blanks.**

Example:

1. 74 ___7___ tens ___4___ ones

2. 96 _____ tens _____ ones

3. 4 tens 3 ones _____

4. 7 tens 8 ones _____

5. 10 tens 0 ones _____

6. 33 _____ tens _____ ones

7. 50 _____ tens _____ ones

8. 6 ones 2 tens _____

9. 2 ones 5 tens _____

10. 38 _____ tens _____ ones

11. 49 _____ tens _____ ones

12. 6 ones 6 tens _____

13. 3 tens 5 ones _____

14. 100 _____ tens _____ ones

Mixed Practice Review: 2-Digit Addition or Subtraction

Solve the problems below.

1.	$\begin{array}{r} 48 \\ -\ 22 \\ \hline \end{array}$	$\begin{array}{r} 38 \\ +\ 11 \\ \hline \end{array}$	$\begin{array}{r} 16 \\ +\ 23 \\ \hline \end{array}$	$\begin{array}{r} 32 \\ -\ 12 \\ \hline \end{array}$	$\begin{array}{r} 86 \\ -\ 66 \\ \hline \end{array}$	$\begin{array}{r} 29 \\ -\ 18 \\ \hline \end{array}$
2.	$\begin{array}{r} 30 \\ +\ 30 \\ \hline \end{array}$	$\begin{array}{r} 20 \\ +\ 18 \\ \hline \end{array}$	$\begin{array}{r} 67 \\ -\ 42 \\ \hline \end{array}$	$\begin{array}{r} 44 \\ +\ 22 \\ \hline \end{array}$	$\begin{array}{r} 89 \\ -\ 63 \\ \hline \end{array}$	$\begin{array}{r} 21 \\ +\ 21 \\ \hline \end{array}$
3.	$\begin{array}{r} 99 \\ +\ 30 \\ \hline \end{array}$	$\begin{array}{r} 24 \\ +\ 24 \\ \hline \end{array}$	$\begin{array}{r} 51 \\ +\ 40 \\ \hline \end{array}$	$\begin{array}{r} 88 \\ -\ 11 \\ \hline \end{array}$	$\begin{array}{r} 67 \\ +\ 22 \\ \hline \end{array}$	$\begin{array}{r} 74 \\ -\ 62 \\ \hline \end{array}$
4.	$\begin{array}{r} 63 \\ -\ 53 \\ \hline \end{array}$	$\begin{array}{r} 49 \\ -\ 21 \\ \hline \end{array}$	$\begin{array}{r} 87 \\ -\ 63 \\ \hline \end{array}$	$\begin{array}{r} 10 \\ +\ 40 \\ \hline \end{array}$	$\begin{array}{r} 11 \\ +\ 82 \\ \hline \end{array}$	$\begin{array}{r} 74 \\ -\ 32 \\ \hline \end{array}$
5.	$\begin{array}{r} 42 \\ +\ 23 \\ \hline \end{array}$	$\begin{array}{r} 51 \\ -\ 30 \\ \hline \end{array}$	$\begin{array}{r} 12 \\ +\ 36 \\ \hline \end{array}$	$\begin{array}{r} 38 \\ -\ 31 \\ \hline \end{array}$	$\begin{array}{r} 75 \\ -\ 42 \\ \hline \end{array}$	$\begin{array}{r} 80 \\ +\ 26 \\ \hline \end{array}$
6.	$\begin{array}{r} 16 \\ +\ 23 \\ \hline \end{array}$	$\begin{array}{r} 60 \\ -\ 20 \\ \hline \end{array}$	$\begin{array}{r} 39 \\ -\ 24 \\ \hline \end{array}$	$\begin{array}{r} 82 \\ +\ 12 \\ \hline \end{array}$	$\begin{array}{r} 96 \\ -\ 43 \\ \hline \end{array}$	$\begin{array}{r} 84 \\ -\ 2 \\ \hline \end{array}$
7.	$\begin{array}{r} 36 \\ +\ 3 \\ \hline \end{array}$	$\begin{array}{r} 42 \\ -\ 31 \\ \hline \end{array}$	$\begin{array}{r} 15 \\ +\ 72 \\ \hline \end{array}$	$\begin{array}{r} 62 \\ -\ 31 \\ \hline \end{array}$	$\begin{array}{r} 68 \\ -\ 60 \\ \hline \end{array}$	$\begin{array}{r} 28 \\ +\ 61 \\ \hline \end{array}$

Mixed Practice Review: Addition or Subtraction 0 — 18

Solve the problems below.

1.

$$\begin{array}{r} 12 \\ -12 \\ \hline \end{array} \qquad \begin{array}{r} 10 \\ -4 \\ \hline \end{array} \qquad \begin{array}{r} 8 \\ +9 \\ \hline \end{array} \qquad \begin{array}{r} 6 \\ -2 \\ \hline \end{array} \qquad \begin{array}{r} 13 \\ -1 \\ \hline \end{array} \qquad \begin{array}{r} 9 \\ -7 \\ \hline \end{array}$$

2.

$$\begin{array}{r} 7 \\ -0 \\ \hline \end{array} \qquad \begin{array}{r} 4 \\ +13 \\ \hline \end{array} \qquad \begin{array}{r} 1 \\ +15 \\ \hline \end{array} \qquad \begin{array}{r} 17 \\ -7 \\ \hline \end{array} \qquad \begin{array}{r} 2 \\ +3 \\ \hline \end{array} \qquad \begin{array}{r} 5 \\ +4 \\ \hline \end{array}$$

3.

$$\begin{array}{r} 3 \\ +7 \\ \hline \end{array} \qquad \begin{array}{r} 3 \\ +5 \\ \hline \end{array} \qquad \begin{array}{r} 9 \\ -2 \\ \hline \end{array} \qquad \begin{array}{r} 11 \\ +7 \\ \hline \end{array} \qquad \begin{array}{r} 4 \\ +2 \\ \hline \end{array} \qquad \begin{array}{r} 3 \\ -1 \\ \hline \end{array}$$

4.

$$\begin{array}{r} 8 \\ -6 \\ \hline \end{array} \qquad \begin{array}{r} 15 \\ +2 \\ \hline \end{array} \qquad \begin{array}{r} 10 \\ -7 \\ \hline \end{array} \qquad \begin{array}{r} 6 \\ -4 \\ \hline \end{array} \qquad \begin{array}{r} 7 \\ +2 \\ \hline \end{array} \qquad \begin{array}{r} 6 \\ +3 \\ \hline \end{array}$$

5.

$$\begin{array}{r} 7 \\ +0 \\ \hline \end{array} \qquad \begin{array}{r} 3 \\ +5 \\ \hline \end{array} \qquad \begin{array}{r} 5 \\ +12 \\ \hline \end{array} \qquad \begin{array}{r} 14 \\ -9 \\ \hline \end{array} \qquad \begin{array}{r} 2 \\ -2 \\ \hline \end{array} \qquad \begin{array}{r} 0 \\ +6 \\ \hline \end{array}$$

6.

$$\begin{array}{r} 11 \\ +0 \\ \hline \end{array} \qquad \begin{array}{r} 11 \\ -5 \\ \hline \end{array} \qquad \begin{array}{r} 4 \\ +14 \\ \hline \end{array} \qquad \begin{array}{r} 5 \\ +9 \\ \hline \end{array} \qquad \begin{array}{r} 15 \\ -10 \\ \hline \end{array} \qquad \begin{array}{r} 16 \\ -8 \\ \hline \end{array}$$

7.

$$\begin{array}{r} 3 \\ +12 \\ \hline \end{array} \qquad \begin{array}{r} 17 \\ -8 \\ \hline \end{array} \qquad \begin{array}{r} 9 \\ -0 \\ \hline \end{array} \qquad \begin{array}{r} 12 \\ -1 \\ \hline \end{array} \qquad \begin{array}{r} 2 \\ +0 \\ \hline \end{array} \qquad \begin{array}{r} 5 \\ +8 \\ \hline \end{array}$$

Mixed Practice Review: Facts 0 — 18

Fill in the blanks with the sum or difference. The first one is done for you.

1. $0 + 13$ = $\underline{13}$	**2.** $11 + 5$ = _____	**3.** $3 + 0$ = _____
$10 - 4$ = _____	$10 - 5$ = _____	$16 + 2$ = _____
$2 + 11$ = _____	$12 - 3$ = _____	$7 + 3$ = _____
$9 + 6$ = _____	$8 + 9$ = _____	$9 - 8$ = _____
$18 - 9$ = _____	$2 + 10$ = _____	$8 - 1$ = _____
$7 + 8$ = _____	$0 + 11$ = _____	$17 - 10$ = _____
4. $11 - 6$ = _____	**5.** $0 - 0$ = _____	**6.** $8 + 10$ = _____
$12 - 5$ = _____	$0 + 9$ = _____	$11 - 11$ = _____
$15 + 3$ = _____	$10 + 0$ = _____	$9 + 8$ = _____
$18 + 0$ = _____	$10 - 0$ = _____	$8 - 1$ = _____
$11 - 9$ = _____	$17 - 0$ = _____	$11 - 1$ = _____
$7 + 5$ = _____	$9 + 0$ = _____	$3 + 2$ = _____
7. $10 + 3$ = _____	**8.** $17 - 15$ = _____	**9.** $13 - 4$ = _____
$5 + 13$ = _____	$10 + 8$ = _____	$10 + 2$ = _____
$7 + 5$ = _____	$11 - 0$ = _____	$0 + 12$ = _____
$6 + 6$ = _____	$9 + 1$ = _____	$18 - 11$ = _____
$17 - 5$ = _____	$11 - 4$ = _____	$3 + 0$ = _____
$12 - 6$ = _____	$6 + 5$ = _____	$8 - 8$ = _____

Keeping Up. Follow the instructions below.

first

1. Color the third and tenth cars blue.

2. Color the ninth and first cars green.

3. Color the fifth and seventh cars brown.

4. Color the second and fourth cars red.

5. Color the sixth and eighth cars black.

Answer Key

Diagnostic Test

Page 5

1. C **2.** A **3.** C **4.** A **5.** B **6.** B **7.** C **8.** C **9.** C **10.** 7, 1, 12, 3 **11.** A **12.** A.

Page 6

13. A **14.** B **15.** A **16.** A **17.** B **18.** A **19.** A **20.** C **21.** A **22.** A **23.** B **24.** B **25.** C **26.** A.

Page 7

27. B **28.** B **29.** C **30.** A **31.** B **32.** C **33.** A **34.** B **35.** A **36.** C **37.** D.

Page 8

38. A **39.** A **40.** A **41.** A **42.** A **43.** A **44.** B **45.** C **46.** B **47.** B **48.** B **49.** B **50.** A.

Page 10

Numbers should match examples but handwriting styles may vary.

Page 11

1. 4 **2.** 0 **3.** 9 **4.** 11 **5.** 3 **6.** 7 **7.** 12 **8.** 8 **9.** 10.

Page 12

1. 8 **2.** 6 **3.** 2 **4.** 12 **5.** 1 **6.** 11 **7.** 5 **8.** 10 **9.** 0.

Page 13

1st Table: Say each numeral out loud as you touch them. **2nd Table:** 1, 2, 3, 4, 5, 6, 7, 8, 9, 10, 11, 12, 13, 14, 15, 16, 17, 18, 19, 20; **3rd Table:** 1, 2, 3, 4, 5, 6, 7, 8, 9, 10, 11, 12, 13, 14, 15, 16, 17, 18, 19, 20. **Draw 20 Objects:** Children should draw 20 objects of their choice.

Page 14

1. 9, 6; **2.** 11, 10; **3.** 7, 8; **4.** 7, 5; **5.** 8, 10; **6.** 12, 9; **7.** Seven circles should be drawn. **Brainworks: The following numbers should be circled:** 6, 8, 4, 0, 2, 9, 1.

Page 15

1	2	3	4	5	6	7	8	9	10
11	12	13	14	15	16	17	18	19	20
21	22	23	24	25	26	27	28	29	30
31	32	33	34	35	36	37	38	39	40
41	42	43	44	45	46	47	48	49	50
51	52	53	54	55	56	57	58	59	60
61	62	63	64	65	66	67	68	69	70
71	72	73	74	75	76	77	78	79	80
81	82	83	84	85	86	87	88	89	90
91	92	93	94	95	96	97	98	99	100

Page 16

Before: 9, 5, 11, 20, 37, 13, 2, 66, 48, 7, 99;
Between: 1, 26, 72, 20, 86, 50, 94, 100, 14, 59, 11;
After: 90, 18, 30, 81, 20, 78, 40, 94, 22, 67, 16.

Page 17

Number words: Listed from left to right, top to bottom. five, four, twelve, eight, seven, two, zero, nine, ten, three, one, eleven, six. **Table: 1.** eight **2.** twelve **3.** four **4.** seven **5.** eleven **6.** five.

Page 18

A. 1-nine **B.** 2-sixes **C.** 3-ones **D.** 4-sevens **E.** 5-eights **F.** 6-tens **G.** 7-threes **H.** 8-zeros **I.** 9-fours **J.** 10-elevens **K.** 11-fives **L.** 12-twos **M.** 0-twelves. **Brainworks: Listed from left to right, top to bottom.** 0, 7, 11, 5, 12, 2, 8, 1, 10, 6, 4, 3, 9.

Page 19

1. two **2.** eight **3.** one and three **4.** eleven **5.** one **6.** seven and nine **7.** two and four **8.** eight **9.** three **10.** eleven **11.** two **12.** three **13.** five and seven **14.** nine **15.** six **16.** twelve **17.** eight and ten **18.** six **19.** four **20.** zero.

Page 20

1. five, 5; **2.** four, 4; **3.** six, 6; **4.** two, 2. **Brainworks: Listed from left to right, top to bottom.** 4, 2, 6, 6, 4, 6, 2, 5, 6, 5, 5, 3.

Page 21

1. 4+1=5 **2.** 3+2=5 **3.** 3+3=6 **4.** 6+0=6 **5.** 2+1=3 **6.** 1+5=6.

Brainworks: Listed from left to right, top to bottom.
1+1=2, 2+3=5, 4+0=4, 3+3=6, 4+0=4, 1+2=3, 2+2=4, 2+1=3, 0+3=3, 5+1=6, 0+0=0, 1+4=5.

Page 22
1. 3, 5, 2; 2. 6, 5, 0; 3. 4, 6, 6; 4. 1, 5, 4, 2, 6; 5. 6, 4, 4, 3, 5; 6. 2, 5, 6, 3, 6; 7. 1, 5, 3, 4, 6; 8. 4+2=6, 3+3=6, 1+2=3; 9. 1+1=2, 3+1=4, 2+0=2; 10. 3+2=5, 1+4=5, 1+5=6; 11. 1+4=5, 1+2=3, 3+0=3; 12. 2+2=4, 0+6=6, 1+3=4.

Page 23
1. 3 / +2 / 5   2. 4+2=6   3. 1+3=4   4. 2 / +1 / 3
5. 4 / +0 / 4   6. 5 / +1 / 6   7. 6 and 3+3=6   8. 0+3=3
9. 1 / +4 / 5   10. 6 / +0 / 6

Page 24
1. 1 2. 4 3. 1 4. 4 5. 2 6. 4 7. 5 8. 3.

Page 25
1. 3-1=2 2. 2-1=1 3. 4-4=0 4. 3-2=1 5. 5-2=3 6. 4-2=2 7. 6-3=3 8. 2-0=2 9. 6-1=5 10. 6-5=1.
Keeping Up: 10, 11, 12, 13, 14, 15, 16, 17, 18; 2. 13, 14, 15, 16, 17, 18, 19, 20.

Page 26
1. 1, 2, 4; 2. 0, 0, 0; 3. 2, 3, 2; 4. 1, 0, 1; 5. 4, 1, 0, 1, 2, 1; 6. 0, 3, 4, 1, 0, 2; 7. 6, 2, 0, 4, 3, 2; 8. 2, 5, 5, 3, 2, 2. **Dot-to-Dot:** The picture is a fish!

Page 27

6	-
0	6
4	2
6	0
3	3
1	5
5	1
2	4

5	-
4	1
2	3
0	5
5	0
1	4
3	2

4	-
2	2
4	0
1	3
3	1
0	4

1	-
0	1
1	0

2	-
2	0
1	1
0	2

3	-
1	2
3	0
0	3
2	1

Brainworks: 6-2=4 still in the pond.

Page 28
1. 2-1=1   2. 4 / -2 / 2   3. 5 / -3 / 2   4. 6-4=2
5. 6-0=6   6. 5-2=3   7. 6 / -3 / 3   8. 3 / -2 / 1

Page 29
1. 4, 6, 3, 6, 5, 4; 2. 2, 0, 1, 3, 4, 2; 3. 5, 4, 2, 0, 5, 2; 4. 0, 5, 5, 5, 4, 6; 5. 2, 0, 4, 1, 4, 0; 6. 6, 2, 3, 1, 3, 2; 7. 3, 4, 1, 6, 1, 6.

Page 30
1. 1+2, 3-1, 2+2, 4-1, 3+3, 6 end; 2. 3+2, 5-1, 4-2, 2+4, 6-3, 3+1, 4-2, 2+3, 5+1, 6-3, 3 end; 3. 0+0, 0+5, 5-4, 1+1, 2-0, 2+2, 4-3, 1+4, 5-5, 0 end; 4. start 6-4, 2+1, 3-0, 3+1, 4+1, 5-1, 4+1, 5+0, 5-0, 5 end.

Page 31
Order may vary. 1. 1+3=4, 3+1=4, 4-3=1, 4-1=3; 2. 3+2=5, 2+3=5, 5-2=3, 5-3=2; 3. 1+2=3, 2+1=3, 3-2=1, 3-1=2; 4. 2+4=6, 4+2=6, 6-4=2, 6-2=4. **Brainworks:** 1. 12, 6 2. 7, 11, 10.

Page 32
1. 5-five 2. 8-eight 3. 3-three 4. 10-ten 5. 12-twelve 6. 9-nine.

Page 33
1. 4-four 2. zero-0 3. eight-8 4. 1-one 5. 11-eleven 6. 6-six 7. 7-seven 8. 5-five 9. 2-two. **Brainworks:** 1. 17 2. 20 3. 14 4. 16 5. 18 6. 15 7. 19 8. 13.

Page 34
1. orange 2. red 3. 7 4. blue and yellow 5. 3 6. 6 7. 4+2=6 8. 6-4=2 9. Answers will vary. 10. 41.

Page 35
1. 2+5=7 2. 4+5=9 3. 8+3=11 4. 7+0=7 5. 6+4=10 6. 1+8=9 7. 9+3=12 8. 5+5=10 9. 3+4=7 10. 0+11=11.

Page 36
Answers are top to bottom for each numbered box.
1. 8, 11, 9, 7, 10, 12; 2. 7, 9, 11, 12, 8, 10; 3. 8, 10, 12, 9, 7, 11; 4. 11, 12, 9, 8, 10, 7; 5. 12, 9, 11, 8, 7, 10; 6. 10, 11, 8, 12, 7, 9; 7. 11, 7, 10, 12, 8, 9; 8. 10, 8, 12, 9, 11, 7; 9. 12, 10, 8, 11, 7, 9; 10. 12, 10, 8, 11, 9; 11. 12, 10, 11, 8, 9; 12. 9, 12, 11, 10, 8.

Page 37
1. 4+5=9   2. 8+2=10   3. 3+8=11   4. 1 / +7 / 8
5. 6 / +6 / 12   6. 5 / +2 / 7

Keeping Up: Answers are left to right, top to bottom.
25, 20, 99, 49, 67, 82, 78, 51, 60, 15, 40, 11, 22, 1, 34.

Page 38
1. 11, 12, 11, 12, 10, 11; **2.** 7, 7, 8, 8, 9, 9; **3.** 11, 12, 11, 8, 10, 12; **4.** 9, 9, 9, 10, 12, 11; **5.** 12, 12, 11, 11, 10, 11; **6.** 9, 7, 11, 10, 11, 8. **Odd or Even:** The following should be circled: 1, 3, 5, 7, 9, 11; **The following should be crossed out:** 2, 4, 6, 8, 10, 12.

Page 39
7-blue: 3+4, 2+5, 0+7, 5+2, 4+3; **8-purple:** 0+8, 2+6, 7+1, 3+5, 6+2, 5+3, 4+4; **9-yellow:** 2+7, 6+3, 1+8, 7+2, 9+0, 3+6; **10-orange:** 8+2, 3+7, 4+6, 10+0, 5+5, 9+1, 7+3, 6+4; **11-green:** 7+4, 9+2, 1+10, 8+3, 6+5, 3+8, 11+0; **12-pink:** 9+3, 6+6, 7+5, 3+9, 4+8, 11+1.

Page 40
1. 3 **2.** 7 **3.** 11-5=6 **4.** 8-3=5 **5.** 5 **6.** 6 **7.** 12-4=8

8. 11
       -7
       4

9. 10
       -6
       4

10. 12
        -2
        10

Page 41
Answers are top to bottom for each numbered box.
1. 8, 7, 2, 3, 1, 0; **2.** 10, 0, 3, 6, 5, 8; **3.** 7, 4, 3, 1, 10, 5; **4.** 4, 6, 2, 0, 3, 5; **5.** 0, 5, 7, 2, 1, 4; **6.** 1, 2, 12, 4, 1, 4; **7.** 11, 9, 7, 1, 5, 4; **8.** 3, 8, 11, 10, 1, 3; **9.** 5, 0, 9, 2, 10, 8; **10.** 2, 4, 8, 9, 8; **11.** 6, 10, 5, 8, 0; **12.** 6, 4, 3, 9, 5.

Page 42
1. 7 **2.** 3 **3.** 2 **4.** 7 **5.** 2 **6.** 2 **7.** 9 **8.** 2 **9.** 9 **10.** 3 **11.** 3 **12.** 4 **13.** 10 **14.** 0 **15.** 3 **16.** 3 **17.** 7 **18.** 6 **19.** 0 **20.** 1 **21.** 5.

Page 43
The underlined problems should be circled.
1. 10-2=8, 10-1=9, <u>11-3=8</u>, 11-0=11, <u>12-4=8</u>, <u>8-0=8</u>; **2.** 7-2=5, <u>12-3=9</u>, <u>10-1=9</u>, <u>11-2=9</u>, 10-8=2, <u>9-0=9</u>; **3.** <u>8-1=7</u>, <u>9-2=7</u>, 10-5=5, 7-4=3, <u>11-4=7</u>, <u>12-5=7</u>; **4.** 12-1=11, 12-6=6, 11-2=9, <u>12-0=12</u>; **5.** <u>11-1=10</u>, 10-10=0, <u>10-0=10</u>, <u>12-2=10</u>; **6.** 11-6=5, <u>12-1=11</u>, <u>11-0=11</u>, 12-9=3; **7.** <u>8-2=6</u>, 9-5=4, <u>10-4=6</u>, 12-7=5, <u>11-5=6</u>, 12-10=2; **8.** 2-2=0, <u>9-5=4</u>, <u>11-7=4</u>, 8-2=6, <u>10-6=4</u>, <u>12-8=4</u>; **9.** <u>11-6=5</u>, <u>9-4=5</u>, <u>7-2=5</u>, 10-3=7, <u>8-3=5</u>, <u>12-7=5</u>. **Keeping Up:** Answers are from left to right, top to bottom. 12, 9, 11, 1, 4, 7, 8, 5.

Page 44
1. 12-4=8 **2.** 7-5=2 **3.** 9-4=5 **4.** 12-6=6 **5.** 11-8=3 **6.** 8-2=6 **7.** 10-3=7 **8.** 12-9=3.

Page 45
1. 4, 8, 0, 8, 3, 6; **2.** 6, 2, 4, 0, 9, 0; **3.** 5, 5, 7, 5, 5, 2; **4.** 4, 1, 11, 2, 2, 4; **5.** 3, 12, 9, 6, 6, 7; **6.** 4, 7, 5, 11, 2, 7. **Brainworks:** 5.

Page 46
1. 3 **2.** 6 **3.** 8 **4.** 1 **5.** 9. **Keeping Up:** 2, 3, 10, 12, 6, 9, 0, 8.

Page 47
1. 1 ten, 2 ones; **2.** 1 ten, 4 ones; **3.** 1 ten, 5 ones; **4.** 1 ten, 0 ones; **5.** 1 ten 7 ones; **6.** 1 ten, 3 ones. **Keeping Up:** Answers are left to right, top to bottom. 41, 9, 95, 30, 37, 19, 39, 17, 13, 65, 15, 89, 79, 6.

Page 48
1. 1 ten, 3 ones; **2.** 2 tens, 5 ones; **3.** 2 tens, 1 one; **4.** 1 ten, 6 ones; **5.** 2 tens, 8 ones; **6.** 2 tens, 2 ones; **7.** 3 tens, 4 ones; **8.** 1 ten, 9 ones; **9.** 1 ten, 7 ones; **10.** 2 tens, 0 ones.

Page 49
1. 3 tens, 4 ones; **2.** 4 tens, 6 ones; **3.** 4 tens, 8 ones; **4.** 2 tens, 7 ones; **5.** 3 tens, 9 ones; **6.** 5 tens, 3 ones; **7.** 1 ten, 5 ones = 15; **8.** 3 tens, 6 ones = 36; **9.** 2 tens, 7 ones = 27; **10.** 2 tens, 3 ones = 23; **11.** 3 tens, 0 ones = 30.

Page 50
1. thru 4. Pictures will vary. **5.** 4 tens, 6 ones; **6.** 2 tens, 3 ones; **7.** 1 ten, 6 ones; **8.** 5 tens, 1 one; **9.** 3 ones, 8 tens; **10.** 23 **11.** 41 **12.** 84 **13.** 52 **14.** 77. **Brainworks:** The following should be circled because they are greater: **15.** 7 tens, 2 ones; **16.** 8 tens, 4 ones; **17.** 9 tens, 6 ones; **18.** 5 tens, 3 ones; **19.** 9 tens, 9 ones; **20.** 4 tens, 6 ones.

Page 51
1. 3 o'clock **2.** 7 o'clock **3.** 6 o'clock **4.** 11 o'clock **5.** 1 o'clock **6.** 12 o'clock. **Brainworks:** 12:00 noon, 12:00 midnight, 12:00 noon.

Page 52
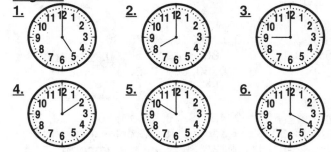

Keeping Up: 9, 9, 11, 12, 12, 12, 12.

Page 53
1. 7:30; **2.** 11:30; **3.** 4:30; **4.** 8:30; **5.** 12:30; **6.** 10:30
7. 5:30; **8.** 6:30. **Brainworks:** 2:00, 12:00.

Page 54
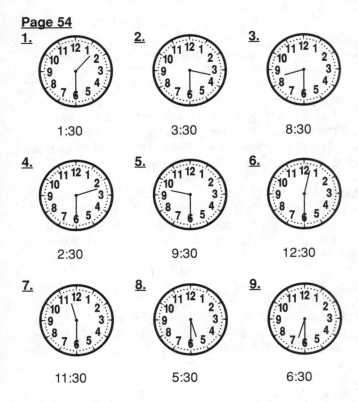

1. 1:30 **2.** 3:30 **3.** 8:30
4. 2:30 **5.** 9:30 **6.** 12:30
7. 11:30 **8.** 5:30 **9.** 6:30

Page 55
A. 9:30 **B.** 8:00 **C.** 12:00 **D.** 6:00 **E.** 1:30 **F.** 4:30
G. 7:30 **H.** 1:00 **I.** 9:00 **J.** 12:30.

Page 56
1. 9:00 **2.** 2:30 **3.** 7:00 **4.** 8:30 **5.** 12:30 **6.** 6:00
7. 4:00 **8.** 10:30 **9.** 1:00 **10.** 11:30 **11.** 6:30 **12.** 9:30
13. 3:30 **14.** 5:00 **15.** 1:30 **16.** 12:00.

Page 57
The following numbers should be shaded: 0, 2, 4, 6,
8, 10, 12, 14, 16, 18, 20, 22, 24, 26, 28, 30, 32, 34, 36,
38, 40, 42, 44, 46, 48, 50, 52, 54. **The same numbers
should be written at the bottom.**

Page 58
Counting by 5's: 0, 5, 10, 15, 20, 25, 30, 35, 40, 45,
50, 55, 60, 65, 70, 75, 80, 85, 90, 95, 100; **Counting by
10's:** 0, 10, 20, 30, 40, 50, 60, 70, 80, 90, 100.

Page 59
Counting by 2's: 2, 4, 6, 8, 10, 12, 14, 16, 18, 20, 22,
24, 26, 28, 30, 32. **Keeping Up: Greater numbers:**
32, 14, 42, 61, 11, 69, 24, 99; **Lesser numbers:** 1, 25,
90, 48, 20, 17, 84, 99.

Page 60
Counting by 5's: 5, 10, 15, 20, 25, 30, 35, 40, 45, 50,
55, 60, 65, 70, 75, 80. **Off Track:** 7 squares, 10 triangles, 6 circles, 3 rectangles, 29 shapes in all.

Page 61
Counting by 10's: 10, 20, 30, 40, 50, 60, 70, 80, 90,
100; **Counting by 5's:** 45¢ **Counting by 2's:** 20¢
Counting by 10's: 90¢.

Page 62
Counting by 2's: 0, 2, 4, 6, 8, 10, 12, 14, 16, 18, 20,
22, 24, 26, 28, 30, 32, 34, 36, 38, 40, 42, 44, 46, 48, 50;
Counting by 10's: 0, 10, 20, 30, 40, 50, 60, 70, 80, 90,
100; **Counting by 5's:** 0, 5, 10, 15, 20, 25, 30, 35, 40,
45, 50, 55, 60, 65, 70, 75, 80, 85, 90, 95, 100.
Keeping Up: 6:00, 4:30, 9:00, 1:30.

Page 63
1. 8+5=13 **2.** 7+10=17 **3.** 10+4=14 **4.** 8+8=16
5. 3+15=18 **6.** 12+5=17 **7.** 6+9=15 **8.** 11+3=14
9. 9+4=13 **10.** 12+6=18. **Brainworks:** A birthday year.

Page 64
1. 15+2=17 **2.** 8+7=15 **3.** 11+5=16 **4.** 6+8=14
5. 4+14=18 **6.** 3+10=13 **7.** 13+0=13 **8.** 1+14=15
9. 8+9=17 **10.** 5+11=16.

Page 65
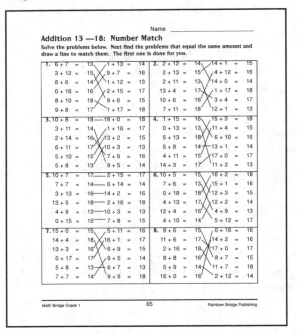

Page 66
1. 14, 15, 18, 17, 14, 13; **2.** 16, 18, 17, 13, 16, 16;
3. 14, 18, 17, 18, 14, 13; **4.** 16, 15, 13, 18, 16, 14; **5.** 13,

15, 18, 17, 18, 16; **6.** 13, 16, 18, 15, 17, 13; **7.** 16, 13, 18, 18, 15, 14.

Page 67
1. 3+10=13 **2.** 4+11=15 **3.** 5+12=17 **4.** 2+13=15
5. 8+7=15 **6.** 8+9=17

7.   9   **8.**   11
     <u>+5</u>   <u>+5</u>
     14   16

Page 68
1. 15-5=10 **2.** 14-7=7 **3.** 17-8=9 **4.** 16-5=11 **5.** 13-9=4
6. 18-13=5 **7.** 15-11=4 **8.** 14-2=12 **9.** 16-10=6
10. 13-9=4 **11.** 14-12=2 **12.** 18-4=14.

Page 69
The underlined problems should be circled.
1. <u>15-7=8</u>, 14-9=5, <u>14-6=8</u>, <u>18-10=8</u>, 17-4=13, <u>17-9=8</u>;
2. <u>18-14=4</u>, <u>13-9=4</u>, 15-8=7, <u>16-12=4</u>, 15-10=5, 14-0=14;
3. 18-18=0, <u>18-8=10</u>, 15-0=15, <u>16-6=10</u>, <u>14-4=10</u>, <u>13-3=10</u>; **4.** <u>16-3=13</u>, <u>13-0=13</u>, <u>18-5=13</u>, <u>15-2=13</u>, 16-2=14, 13-2-11; **5.** 16-13=3, <u>16-16=0</u>, 15-0=15, <u>13-13=0</u>, 18-7=11, <u>17-17=0</u>; **6.** <u>18-16=2</u>, 16-9=7, <u>15-13=2</u>, 14-8=6, <u>13-11=2</u>, 17-16=1; **7.** <u>17-16=1</u>, 15-13=2, <u>14-13=1</u>, <u>16-15=1</u>, <u>18-17=1</u>, 17-12=5; **8.** <u>14-9=5</u>, 15-0=15, 13-1=12, <u>16-11=5</u>, <u>17-12=5</u>, <u>13-8=5</u>;
9. 17-15=2, 18-18=0, <u>17-6=11</u>, <u>15-4=11</u>, <u>13-2=11</u>, 14-0=14.

Page 70
1. 12, 4, 10, 11, 7, 9; **2.** 0, 12, 12, 6, 6, 7; **3.** 6, 9, 13, 3, 0, 7; **4.** 6, 17, 8, 8, 12, 3; **5.** 7, 9, 18, 10, 11, 15; **6.** 9, 12, 2, 16, 14, 3; **7.** 7, 14, 16, 6, 3, 1.

Page 71
Blue: 17-0, 18-1; **Red:** 17-4, 14-1; **Black:** 16-10, 18-12; **Green:** 15-14, 18-17; **Orange:** 17-13 **Yellow:** 18-3, 18-3, 16-1, 16-1, 15-0, 17-2.

Page 72
1. 16-3=13 **2.** 14-6=8 **3.** 13-5=8 **4.** 15-7=8 **5.** 16-9=7
6. 18-12=6 **7.** 13-6=7 **8.** 17-4=13 **9.** 14-5=9 **10.** 18-9=9
11. 15-4=11 **12.** 17-13=4.

Page 73
1. 6, 14, 8, 9, 1, 10; **2.** 8, 6, 9, 13, 3, 9; **3.** 5, 5, 10, 1, 0, 9; **4.** 8, 6, 5, 7, 8, 0; **5.** 12, 6, 11, 10, 5, 9; **6.** 13, 10, 14, 2, 11, 4. **Keeping Up:** 5, 10, 15, 20, 25, 30, 35, 40, 45, 50, 55, 60, 65, 70, 75.

Page 74
1. 5, 7, 15, 7, 13, 14; **2.** 12, 1, 8, 6, 2, 11; **3.** 3, 7, 10, 14, 2, 3; **4.** 12, 10, 12, 13, 3, 1; **5.** 15, 7, 4, 4, 2, 3; **6.** 17, 12, 15, 5, 2, 7; **7.** 10, 14, 4, 3, 18, 9; **8.** 1, 16, 16,

12, 14, 6; **9.** 13, 0, 14, 16, 1, 3; **10.** 11, 13, 16, 2, 0; **11.** 0, 12, 0, 11, 1; **12.** 2, 11, 15, 9, 17.

Page 75
1. 8¢ **2.** 30¢ **3.** 70¢ **4.** 14¢ **5.** 50¢ **6.** 47¢ **7.** 16¢
8. 27¢ **9.** 53¢ **10.** 18¢.

Page 76
Answers may vary. 1. 1 dime, 1 nickel or 3 nickels; **2.** 2 dimes, 1 nickel or 3 nickels, 1 dime; **3.** 2 dimes, 2 nickels, 2 pennies; **4.** 3 nickels, 1 penny; **5.** 3 dimes, 3 nickels; **6.** 2 dimes, 1 nickel,4 pennies or 1 dime, 3 nickels, 4 pennies; **7.** 6 dimes or 5 dimes, 2 nickels **8.** 1 dime, 1 penny or 2 nickels, 1 penny.

Page 77
1. 30¢ **2.** 5¢ **3.** 15¢ **4.** 1¢ **5.** 10¢ **6.** 4 **7.** 1 nickel, 1 penny; **8.** 25¢ **9.** 3 nickels, 1 dime, 1 nickel; **10.** 25¢ **11.** 50¢ **12.** 30¢ **13.** 2 dimes, 1 penny or 21 pennies; **14.** 1 quarter or 2 dimes, 1 nickel; **15.** 10 pennies, 1 dime, 2 nickels. **How much money: 1.** 39¢ **2.** 56¢ **3.** 60¢ **4.** 56¢.

Page 78
A. Truck **B.** Teddy bear **C.** Ball **D.** Necklace **E.** Ring **F.** Drum **G.** Balloon **H.** Doll.

Page 79
1. 10¢+5¢=15¢ **2.** 9¢+4¢=13¢ **3.** 18¢-9¢=9¢
4. 10¢+8¢=18¢ **5.** 15¢-4¢=11¢ **6.** 14¢+3¢=17¢
7. 20¢+5¢=25¢ **8.** 16¢-8¢=8¢ **9.** 8¢+8¢=16¢
10. 15¢-10¢=5¢ **11.** 6¢+8¢=14¢ **12.** 17¢-9¢=8¢.
Brainworks: 43¢-6¢=37¢.

Page 80
1. 2, 18, 14, 4, 8, 18; **2.** 6, 0, 10, 16, 20, 12; **3.** 14, 2, 22, 10, 4, 8; **4.** 6, 24, 12, 16, 0, 20. **Number Families: Order may vary. 1.** 2+12=14, 12+2=14, 14-12=2, 14-2=12; **2.** 5+11=16, 11+5=16, 16-11=5, 16-5=11; **3.** 10+8=18, 8+10=18, 18-8=10, 18-10=8; **4.** 5+8=13, 8+5=13, 13-8=5, 13-5=8.

Page 81
1. 12, 16, 4, 4, 10, 16; **2.** 4, 7, 15, 13, 16, 11; **3.** 5, 10, 12, 17, 17, 10; **4.** 11, 10, 11, 5, 5, 11; **5.** 17, 8, 8, 18, 10, 5. **Brainworks:**

first   second   third   fourth   fifth

Page 82
1. 2, 1, 1, 2, 1, 8; **2.** 2, 7, 1, 1, 0, 9; **3.** 1, 10, 2, 5, 7, 9; **4.** 3, 0, 3, 4, 0, 11; **5.** 3, 8, 3, 9, 0, 2.

Brainworks: 1. $\frac{1}{3}$ **2.** $\frac{2}{3}$ **3.** $\frac{1}{2}$ **4.** $\frac{3}{4}$ **5.** $\frac{4}{7}$

Page 83
1. 0, 13, 14, 10, 7, 10; **2.** 9, 12, 14, 5, 6, 10; **3.** 6, 3, 11, 9, 9, 12; **4.** 8, 10, 8, 6, 13, 16; **5.** 6, 6, 11, 8, 14, 8; **6.** 9, 14, 15, 14, 2, 4; **7.** 8, 12, 1, 3, 7, 12; **8.** 2, 8, 9, 8, 17, 18; **9.** 4, 3, 12, 7, 12, 18; **Brainworks: 1.** 9 **2.** 3 **3.** 5 **4.** 2 **5.** 10 **6.** 7.

Page 84
1 1, 0, 4, 6, 0, 1; **2.** 5, 5, 11, 2, 4, 4; **3.** 0, 8, 8, 4, 4, 0; **4.** 3, 1, 4, 4, 7, 6; **5.** 6, 2, 12, 0, 9, 8; **6.** 0, 4, 13, 8, 3, 1; **7.** 2, 1, 5, 6, 2, 3; **8.** 6, 3, 3, 1, 16, 5; **9.** 4, 14, 5, 9, 1, 3. **Brainworks: 1.** 2 **2.** 5 **3.** 1 **4.** 3 **5.** 4 **6.** 6.

Page 85
1. 6, 7, 15, 6, 13, 6; **2.** 6, 14, 18, 12, 11, 13; **3.** 9, 14, 15, 13, 9, 8; **4.** 14, 16, 15, 5, 8, 8; **5.** 7, 9, 12, 15, 18, 14; **6.** 12, 10, 15, 17, 17, 11.

Page 86
1. 25, 78, 35, 29, 39, 44; **2.** 21, 58, 55, 67, 63, 26; **3.** 26, 67, 56, 95, 69, 91; **4.** 48, 29, 58, 84, 99, 30; **5.** 99, 78, 29, 90, 59, 20. **Brainworks:** 2+2+4+1+2=11 total inches.

Page 87
1. 13, 22, 20, 47, 61, 11; **2.** 8, 44, 36, 12, 31, 12; **3.** 70, 0, 11, 32, 10, 44; **4.** 41, 11, 17, 33, 72, 21; **5.** 79, 30, 23, 10, 31, 13. **Keeping Up: 1.** 7 tens, 4 ones; **2.** 9 tens, 6 ones; **3.** 43 **4.** 78 **5.** 100 **6.** 3 tens, 3 ones; **7.** 5 tens, 0 ones; **8.** 26 **9.** 52 **10.** 3 tens, 8 ones; **11.** 4 tens, 9 ones; **12.** 66 **13.** 35 **14.** 10 tens, 0 ones.

Page 88
1. 26, 49, 39, 20, 20, 11; **2.** 60, 38, 25, 66, 26, 42; **3.** 129, 48, 91, 77, 89, 12; **4.** 10, 28, 24, 50, 93, 42; **5.** 65, 21, 48, 7, 33, 106; **6.** 39, 40, 15, 94, 53, 82; **7.** 39, 11, 87, 31, 8, 89.

Page 89
1. 0, 6, 17, 4, 12, 2; **2.** 7, 17, 16, 10, 5, 9; **3.** 10, 8, 7, 18, 6, 2; **4.** 2, 17, 3, 2, 9, 9; **5.** 7, 8, 17, 5, 0, 6; **6.** 11, 6, 18, 14, 5, 8; **7.** 15, 9, 9, 11, 2, 13.

Page 90
1. 13, 6, 13, 15, 9, 15; **2.** 16, 5, 9, 17, 12, 11; **3.** 3, 18, 10, 1, 7, 7; **4.** 5, 7, 18, 18, 2, 12; **5.** 0, 9, 10, 10, 17, 9; **6.** 18, 0, 17, 7, 10, 5; **7.** 13, 18, 12, 12, 12, 6; **8.** 2, 18, 11, 10, 7, 11; **9.** 9, 12, 12, 7, 3, 0.
Keeping Up:

green   red   blue   red   brown   black   brown   black   green   blue

www.rainbowbridgepub.com